Rhodes

- A (☞ in the text denotes a highly recommended sight
- A complete A–Z of practical information starts on p.101
- Extensive mapping on cover flaps and in text

Berlitz Publishing Company, Inc.

Princeton Mexico City London Eschborn Singapore

Text: Barbara Ender
Photography: Jurg Donatsch
Layout: Media Content Marketing, Inc.
Cartography: 🔵 Falk-Verlag, Munich

*Although the publisher tries to insure the accuracy of all the
information in this book, changes are inevitable and errors may
result. The publisher cannot be responsible for any resulting loss,
inconvenience, or injury. If you find an error in this guide, please
let the editors know by writing to Berlitz Publishing Company,
400 Alexander Park, Princeton, NJ 08540-6306.*

ISBN 2-8315-6520-0

Revised 1998 – Fourth Printing September 2000

Printed in Switzerland by Weber SA, Bienne
040/009 RP

CONTENTS

RHODES

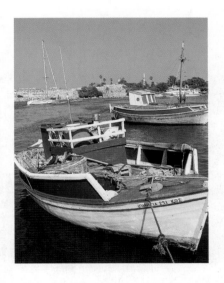

THE ISLAND
AND ITS PEOPLE

There's no escaping the past in Rhodes—it is etched into the very skyline, in the crumbling ruins of ancient temples and crusaders' castles crowning its hills. Round, squat, red-tiled roofs pinpoint Orthodox churches, while severe stone battlements and fanciful lacy trimmings stand reminiscent of the Doge's Palace in Venice—such is Rhodes Town, neatly entrenched in the island's jutting, northern tip.

Whether you approach by air or sea, you'll see at once that this is not a typical Greek island. Rhodes is green, very green —the hills are fragrant with lavender, sage, and marjoram, and even its butterflies have a valley all of their own. More than living up to its name, "the rose" (*ródos*), the island charms visitors with a profusion of scents and colours from the flowers which adorn its courtyards: hibiscus, jasmine, honeysuckle, oleander, and bougainvillaea.

Rhodes is the administrative capital of the Dodecanese archipelago, a long way from its government in Athens (14 hours by express ferry), but just 20 km (12 miles) from the Turkish mainland. The Dodecanese (*dódeka nísi*, "twelve islands"), united in 1908 against discriminatory Turkish legislation, were subsequently joined by Rhodes and Kos.

The group came under Italian rule from the Italo-Turkish war of 1912 until 1947, when they formed a Greek administrative region covering some 200 islands, only 14 of which have any sizeable population. Hugging the Turkish coast, the islands curve round from Pátmos, where St. John the Divine wrote his *Book of Revelation*, down to tiny Kastellórizo far away to the east—so far that it won't fit into any map of Greece. Rhodes is the largest island of the group.

Shoes are just one export; skilled craftsmen have been here for centuries.

Almost half of the 90,000 population is concentrated in Rhodes Town. During ancient times, there were five times as many islanders, a people famed throughout the Aegean for their wealth, culture, and skill as both shipbuilders and traders. Traces of them come to light whenever the foundations are dug for a new hotel. The stadium on Monte Smith, for instance, was used by athletes training for the Olympics centuries before the birth of Christ; the Temple of Apollo still serves as a landmark for sailors, as it did thousands of years ago.

Four centuries of Turkish rule imprinted the island with an exotic air, but the Turkish influence is less esteemed than that of the Italians, who in little over a decade managed to excavate and restore Classical sites, as well as build roads, homes, and public buildings. The strongest cultural impact here, however—and indeed elsewhere in the Dodecanese—remains that of its medieval crusader Knights of St. John, who walled the city and built the massive Grand Masters' Palace as its focal point.

The joy of Rhodes is its smiling climate. Its divine protector is Helios, god of the sun, in residence 300 days a year. Fair-skinned worshippers from darkest northern Europe flock to his island. There's no escaping it—Rhodes is a major destination for tourism, which has brought the mixed blessings of prosperity weighed against the scars of clutches of concrete hotels. In spite of new policies to spread people more evenly along the coast, most beaches have remained crowded. If you come here only for the sun and fun, it would be quite easy to spend two weeks commuting from your hotel to the beach without even realizing that you were in Greece. Shop signs are in English, shopkeepers speak in German, and menus are in every European language.

A colourful, cosmopolitan, and babbling throng bulldozes the narrow, cobbled streets of the old bazaar in the day and crawls the pubs and discos by night. *Bouzoúki* music pulsates from lively *tavérnas* in every direction, and yachts and pleasure boats jostle with caïques for moorings in the harbour.

Nonetheless, it's not difficult to hunt down more secluded spots. Flowery gardens, the back streets of Rhodes Old Town, the historical sites of Líndos, Kámiros, and Iályssos —the island's three ancient trading ports—are enormously rewarding, with many of the roads in the hilly interior still unsurfaced, and in places little more than dirt tracks. You can walk along them for hours and meet no one but an old man and his donkey. The scenery is bewitching—olive groves, gnarled oaks, wind-twisted fig trees, dark ranks of cypresses, fields of poppies and daisies, and orchards of oranges and lemons, boughs often sagging due to the weight of the golden fruit. The only sounds are the call of a cuckoo and the tinkling of a goat bell, or perhaps a stealthy slither in the undergrowth—it's easy to believe that it's a *kaous*, a woodland sprite, the Rhodian Pan.

Rhodes is one of the few Greek islands large enough to make it worthwhile bringing a car. Of course, you could also rent one, or a moped or motorbike; or, if you're with a group,

RHODES AT A GLANCE

Government

Greece is a parliamentary Democratic Republic, with a president elected for a 5-year term. The country is divided into 13 administrative regions, one of which is the Dodecanese, an archipelago of more than 200 islands. Eighteen of these islands are inhabited; Astipalía, Chálki, Kálymnos, Kárpathos, Kásos, Kastellórizo, Kos, Léros, Níssiros, Pátmos, Rhodes, Symi, and Tílos have local governments and comprise what is officially referred to as the Dodecanese islands, with Rhodes, the largest, as the administrative capital. Island governors are appointed by Athens; mayors are elected locally.

Geography

Rhodes is situated 265 nautical miles from Piraeus, and 10 from the Turkish coast. It is crossed northeast and southeast by hills reaching 1,215 metres (3,986 feet) at the summit of Mount Attáviros, which commands a view, on a clear day, as far as the peak of Mount Ida on Crete. Rhodes is greener than the other Dodecanese, with forests of pine, oak, and cypress, olive groves and vineyards, and orange and lemon orchards which are irrigated by a system of windmills exploiting the constant breeze. Its area measures 1,398 square km (540 square miles), and its perimeter 220 km (136 miles), with several sheltered bays on the east side. Rhodes Town forms the northern tip of the island.

Population

The island 90,000; Rhodes Town 43,600.

Economy

Tourism (over 1 million visitors a year), and agriculture: wine, grain, olives, figs, pomegranates, oranges, and lemons.

Language

Demotic Greek. In tourist areas, most people can manage English and perhaps German, Italian, Swedish, and Finnish.

Religion

The official religion is Greek Orthodox.

club together and take a taxi. The buses are very handy for the best-known sites, and they stick more or less to schedule, which is quite amazing when you consider that the driver might well have to call in at a bakery in one village, deliver fish in another, and stop off to chat to friends in a café and have a drink from a curative fountain in yet another. What does time matter?

Stress is unheard of here. Look around you—no long faces, everyone seems happy and full of good humour. Just see them rattling blithely over the cobblestones of the Old Town on their mopeds, three generations on two wheels: father in front, baby in the middle, granny riding side-saddle behind. The noisier, the merrier.

If anything should happen to annoy them, the Greeks fly out immediately, shouting and gesticulating in the street, getting it off their chest and never harbouring a grudge. A crowd gathers round to join in the fun, and in no time everyone is the best of pals again. The legendary Greek hospitality

Children pass away the afternoon hours by playing
backgammon outdoors.

is a reality on this island, revealed by simple gestures like the gift of a full-blown rose, or a few sprigs of basil from a windowsill pot. It's easy to meet people—venture a smile and a *kalimera* ("good morning") and you're already halfway to making a friend.

The Rhodians remain resolutely cheerful in spite of the hordes of tourists who are, after all, their livelihood. They love their island and are proud to show its charms to visitors. Whether leading animated discussions on *tavérna* terraces, sitting in front of their shops clicking worrybeads or jangling their keys, taking a walk along the harbour front, or just playing backgammon with a neighbour, they like to spend most of their time outdoors. Their greatest pleasures come from their family, as well as their surroundings, music, and, of course, dancing.

This appealing way of life is even more apparent in the other Dodecanese islands, all of which are connected with Rhodes by air or sea. When you plan your stay, include some time for a few days on one of these tranquil islands. Kálymnos, home of the famous sponge divers and a mecca for underwater fishing; Kárpathos, where the villagers wear traditional costume for their own comfort rather than for tourist photos; rugged Pátmos, something of an aristocrat, with its handsome coastal villas and private houses up in the capital around the hallowed monastery of St. John the Divine; or Astipalía, remote and still sedate, cultivating a rough chic.

Even more remote are Tílos, Kásos, Níssiros, Kastellórizo, and Léros, which avoid the masses simply by not catering to them. Closer to Rhodes, and perfect for a day trip, are the charming little islands of Symi and Chálki. Kos, pleasant and green out of season, is fun for visitors who prefer their holidays loud and boisterous.

However you like your islands, you're bound to enjoy Rhodes. It's a family island, with plenty to do and see: a delightful old town, an exceptional historical legacy, hundreds of shops, an effervescent nightlife, all the watersports you could want, restaurants offering the best of the world's cuisines, and plenty of places to get away from it all. The hard part is having to choose from such an embarrassment of riches. You could of course just laze like a lizard on the beach, searching for the perfect pebble, or a word to suit the cool, blue sea. Kingfisher? Aquamarine? Peacock?

There is always time to dream—and plenty more for sightseeing tomorrow.

The beautiful landscape of Kámiros stretches down to reach the sea.

A BRIEF HISTORY

From the waters of the sea arose an island
which is held by the father of the piercing beams of light,
the ruler of the steeds whose breath is fire.

Thus Pindar, in his Seventh Ode, described the birth of Rhodes, during ancient times known as Heliousa, the Sun-friend. Helios gave the island to the nymph Rhodon, his favourite, as a place to live. The sun god has always ruled over Rhodes, and the yearly festivals held in his honour were famous throughout the Aegean. A team of four horses was cast into the sea as a sacrifice, symbolizing the sun's daily journey across the sky.

Few traces remain of the first inhabitants, a primitive and rugged people from Asia Minor. We do know, however, that they could produce fire, fashion simple tools, and cast pottery. From 2500–1500 B.C., during the Bronze Age, Carians from Anatolia and Phoenicians from Lebanon settled on the island and then moved west to Crete and beyond. Minoan merchants from Crete set up shop in the ports of Líndos, Kámiros, and Iályssos (named after the grandsons of Helios), to continue lucrative trading with Egypt and the Levant.

The Making of a Nation

The Minoans had been driven from Crete by earthquake and invaders from the Greek mainland, the Achaeans. The Achaeans were the Greeks of Homer's *Iliad*, amphibious warriors who had pushed south through Athens and by 1500 B.C. had attacked and occupied both Crete and Rhodes. When the Achaeans launched their famous 1,000 ships against Troy, according to Homer "nine ships of the arrogant Rhodians" sailed with Agamemnon's fleet. The 10-year war ended with the destruction of Troy, but it also exhausted both the resources and spirit of the conquerors. They were no match for the tall, blond, and savage Dorians from the Balkans, who swept through Greece in 1200 B.C.

The fusion of the Dorians with the Aegean people eventually produced the Classical period of Greek civilization. As for Rhodes, it was encouraged to develop independently as a city-state. By 700 B.C., the three Rhodian cities, together with the Asia Minor ports of Halicarnassus (now Bodrum) and Knidos, and the island of Kos, had set up a six-city trading league under Dorian charter, the Hexapolis. Each city minted its own coins (money had just been invented in Asia Minor), and Líndos dispatched merchants with instructions to colonize Spain's Costa Brava, Gela in Sicily, and Nea Polis in Italy, which is present-day Naples.

On the site of an ancient temple, the Church of our Lady of Filérimos recalls the ancient trading city of Ialyssos.

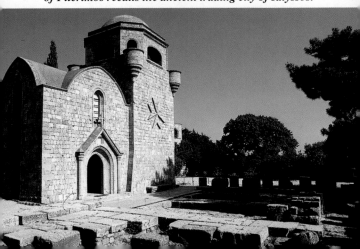

HISTORICAL LANDMARKS

Stone Age Primitive people from Asia Minor inhabit caves.

Bronze Age Carians from Anatolia and Phoenicians from Lebanon settle on island.

1500-1300 B.C. Minoan merchants from Crete installed in ports of Líndos, Kámiros, and Ialyssos. Achaean invaders follow.

1230-25 Capture of Troy.

1200 Dorians sweep through Greece, introducing a dark age of despotism. Rhodes encouraged to develop independently.

700 Hexapolis trading league formed between Halicarnassus and Knidos in Asia Minor, Líndos, Kos, Kámiros, and Ialyssos.

490 Rhodes joins forces with Persian fleet and suffers defeat by Athens at Marathon. Ten years later, the Greeks sink Xerxes' fleet at Salamis, including 40 Rhodian ships.

478 Rhodes becomes taxpaying member of Delian League, under leadership of Athens.

408 The City of Rhodes is founded and prospers with trade.

342 School of Rhetoric founded.

305 Demetrius the Besieger attacks city, but the Rhodians hold out. Hostilities end in a truce.

290 Chares of Líndos completes Colossus, made from left-over battle equipment from Demetrius' siege.

227 The Colossus is toppled by an earthquake.

First century A.D. Stormy alliance with Rome. Sacking of Rhodes by Cassius, who sends 3,000 statues to Italy.

51 St. Paul lands in Líndos, on his way to Syria.

2nd-10th centuries	Rhodes suffers at the hands of Goths, Persians, Arabs, and pirates.
1191	Richard the Lionheart and Philip Augustus land on Rhodes to recruit mercenaries for the Crusades.
1248-1521	Knights of the Order of St. John leave Cyprus and buy Rhodes. They rebuild the Old City, fortifying the ramparts, and fight off Muslim attacks.
1522	Suleiman the Magnificent besieges the city. Rhodians hold out but are finally betrayed.
1523-1912	Rhodes is governed by the Turks, who remain in the city until the eventual fall of the Ottoman Empire.
1912-43	Italy takes hold of the Dodecanese islands and restores ramparts and many old buildings, excavates ancient cities, and rebuilds the New Town.
1945	British forces liberate the Dodecanese from the Germans.
1947	The islands are united with Greece; Rhodes is granted duty-free status.
1950-1990	Hotels and tourist facilities are widely developed in the northern part of Rhodes.
1990	Rhodes Town gains official recognition as a World Heritage Site, protected by UNESCO.

Due to Rhodes' proximity to the east, the Phoenician alphabet was introduced to the island before reaching the rest of Greece, and some of the inscriptions discovered on the island are the earliest existing examples of Greek script.

In the fifth century B.C., a large force dispatched by the king of Persia, Darius, reached the Aegean, where Greece alone stood in the way of its westward drive. Joining up with the Persians, Rhodes suffered defeat with them at Marathon in 490 B.C. When the Greeks sank the fleet of Darius' son, Xerxes, at Salamis 10 years later, there were around 40 Rhodian ships among the victims. The Delian League, under leadership from Athens, was founded soon afterwards, and Rhodes became a taxpaying member.

Sailing before the Wind

Due to its strategic position on vital trade routes in the eastern Mediterranean, close to both Asia Minor and the Middle East, Rhodes grew in importance as a maritime power and centre of finance. It tried to remain neutral, except when its trading interests were at stake, thus supporting first the Delian League and then Persia against Macedonia.

By 408 B.C., the volume of trade and shipping had become too much for the island's three ports to handle, and by mutual consent the City of Rhodes was founded. Well situated at the northern tip of the island, it was the perfect answer, with its five large natural harbours. The design of the wide streets was based on the grid pattern of the famous architect Hippodamus of Miletus, and many of today's thoroughfares, in both Old and New towns, still follow the same plan. The new city prospered and minted its own coins, which showed the head of Helios on one side and the rose of Rhodes on the other. Meanwhile Iályssos and Kámiros declined, eventually becoming little more than centres of religion.

When it became clear that Alexander the Great was worthy of the name, Rhodes sided with him and benefitted from trade concessions with Egypt—Macedonia's next conquest. After the great leader's death in 323 B.C., Rhodes refused to join with an expedition by his successor, Antigonus, against Ptolemy I, the Macedonian general who had become the king of Egypt. This led to an attack on the city in 305 B.C. by Antigonus' son Demetrius, known as "the Besieger."

Demetrius had an army of 40,000 troops, not including the cavalry, engineers, and 170 troopships. But his *pièce de résistance* was the *Helepolis*, a huge, ingenious siege machine nine storeys high, propelled on wheels of oak. Protected by a skin of hides, and with built-in archers' nests, battering rams, grappling hooks, drawbridges, and catapults, it was heaved right up to the ramparts of the fortified city by a crew of 3,400. Inside it were tanks of water, with hosepipes made from cow intestines to quench the flames of burning arrows.

With its first attack the juggernaut broke down a section of the wall, but the troops that poured through it met with ferocious resistance from the Rhodians. Severely damaged, *Helepolis* retreated, and while Demetrius supervised repairs, the Rhodians busied themselves patching up their ramparts and devising a way to foil further attacks. The solution was found by the state architect, Diognetus, who dug a long ditch in the path of the machine. One version of the story claims that he diverted the town's sewage into it, thus bogging down the machine.

The hostilities ended in a truce, with Rhodes accepting an alliance with Antigonus against any enemy other than Ptolemy, and Demetrius holding 100 hostages as a guarantee. He then handed over the remains of his battle equipment to the Rhodians, asking them to sell it and build a commemorative monument of the siege from the proceeds. Thus was born the famous Colossus, one of the Seven Wonders of the Ancient World.

Alliance with Rome

At the peak of its power and with a population about three times that of today, Rhodes enjoyed a golden age in the third century B.C. The island won fame as a cultural and intellectual centre within the Roman Empire, and attracted visitors such as

Gnaeus Pompey, Mark Antony, Cicero, Julius Caesar, Cato the Younger, Cassius, and Brutus to its famous School of Rhetoric, founded in 342 B.C. by the Athenian Aeschines. Rhodian artists and craftsmen, passing on skills from generation to generation, enjoyed a privileged social standing and were regarded highly throughout the Mediterranean. When the Colossus was toppled by an earthquake in 227 B.C., the rest of the city was destroyed too, but such was its prestige in the Hellenistic world that enough financial and technical help was sent in to rebuild it.

In 166 B.C., Rhodes refused to side with Rome against Perseus of Macedonia. As a punishment, Rome took away

Colossal Error

Sorry, contrary to popular belief, the Colossus of Rhodes did not straddle the entrance to Mandráki Harbour. Its 20 tons of bronze would have sunk immediately into the seabed. Instead, more recent theories place the statue of Rhodes' protector, the sun god Helios, near the Palace of the Grand Masters.

Sculptor Chares of Líndos took 12 years to cast the Colossus. Extracting bronze from the *Helepolis* left after Demetrius' siege, he finished his 32 metres (105 feet) masterpiece around 290 B.C. Each finger, we are told, was the size of a man. Despite the fact that his work was considered as one of the Seven Wonders of the Ancient World, Chares committed suicide after discovering a mistake in his calculations. During an earthquake, less than 70 years after its completion, the Colossus cracked at the knees and crashed to the ground.

The Delphic oracle warned the Rhodians not to restore the statue, and the crumpled bronze lay where it had fallen for nearly 900 years. In the mid-seventh century, Arab pirates sacked Rhodes and sold off the bronze as scrap to a Jewish merchant from Syria, who needed 90 camels to carry it (although, of course, legend says it was 900).

The 15th-century Knights' Hospital was built on top of Roman ruins in Rhodes Town.

one of the island's important protectorates, Delos, declaring it a free port and depriving Rhodes of a substantial income from port duties. Therefore, in 164 B.C., Rhodes concluded an alliance with Rome, and from that moment the island was rewarded or punished by Italy in direct accordance with the level of its military support for Rome's constant wars.

The alliance brought a new dilemma for Rhodes—which side it should take in Rome's civil wars and internal struggles. It supported Pompey versus Julius Caesar, but after his defeat of the Rhodians, Caesar forgave them and re-cemented the alliance. Then Cassius and Brutus, the assassins of Caesar, demanded Rhodian help in their war against the senate. When this was refused, Cassius besieged, conquered, and sacked Rhodes. He plundered 3,000 statues and dispatched them to Rome, leaving nothing but "*the sun*"—a famous sculpture by Lysippus of the chariot of Helios, too heavy to remove. Almost all of this precious art was destroyed when Rome burned in July of A.D. 64.

In the Name of God

Christianity took root during the first century, aided by St. Paul, who visited the island on his way to Syria, 20 years after the Crucifixion. However, the island was not to find peace or stability. The City of Rhodes was twice shattered by earthquakes, in A.D. 155 and 515. Much weakened, it became a prime target for armies of invaders. It was plundered by the Goths in A.D. 263, overrun by Persians and Arabs in the seventh century, and unceasingly harassed by pirates and corsairs. Although nominally part of the Byzantine Empire, Rhodes was on its own as far as defence was concerned.

By the 11th century, followers of Muhammad had conquered Jerusalem, implanted their faith in Persia and North Africa, converted the Turks, and occupied more than half of Spain. To Christians, they represented an enormous threat to their faith and to the security of Europe.

Rhodes' ties with Western Europe were strengthened— first through the resumption of trade with Venice, and then, in 1097, with the appearance of the crusaders on their journey to the Holy Land. In 1191, Richard the Lionheart of

England and Philip Augustus of France landed in Rhodes to recruit mercenaries. Constantinople was captured by the crusaders 13 years later. The tide of battle turned, and by 1291 the Christian army was forced off the beaches at Acre (now part of Israel).

Among the retreating soldiers were the Knights of the Order of St. John, founded in Jerusalem more than two centuries earlier. They had run a hospital for pilgrims who succumbed to the hardships of travel. During the Crusades, however, these Knights Hospitallers became more and more militaristic. Forced to fight off repeated Muslim attacks, they

Rhodes from atop its massive ramparts. This sturdy defence system guaranteed safety and now affords fine views.

learned the value of fortified walls, even in the Holy Land. When ordered to regroup, the Knights settled on Cyprus, but as the Muslim threat to that island began to grow, they moved to Rhodes, deciding that it would make a better bastion.

Since the fierce Genoese pirates who had taken Rhodes in 1248 would not let them settle there, the Knights decided to buy the island from them. Although an authentic bill of sale was drawn up, they still had to fight for their newly acquired property, defeating—and subsequently massacring—the Turkish mercenaries assigned by the Byzantine emperor.

By 1309, the Knights had started the elaborate fortification of Rhodes. They settled in, continued to improve the defences, and fought off Muslim assaults for the next 213 years, sometimes carrying the battle to the Turkish mainland. Of course they also maintained a hospital—the Order's *raison d'être* (see page 33).

In their Rhodes bastion, the Knights never numbered over 600, all members of the noblest families in Europe. They took monastic vows of obedience, poverty, and chastity, but their thirst for Muslim blood and hunger for Muslim money and goods was decidedly un-Christian.

Seven "tongues" (later eight, when Spain split into Aragon and Castile) were represented according to native language. These were English, German, French, Provençal, Auvergnat, Spanish, and Italian. Each lived in a compound called an inn, under an appointed prior. For security, they went about in pairs and left the walled domain only on horseback.

Supported by Auvergne and Provence, the French outnumbered the other tongues when it came to electing the lifelong post of Grand Master. Thus, 14 of the 19 Grand Masters were French, and French was the order's spoken language (Latin for official documents). The Italians' natural maritime talents made them the obvious choice to command the fleet, while other tongues each defended a section, or "curtain," of the city walls.

Outside the city, the Knights extended their system of defences with some 30 fortresses strung across the island and yet more on outlying islands, some still to be seen on Kálimnos, Léros, Chálki, Tílos, Kos, Níssiros, and Symi. They were linked by an elaborate communications network of fires, homing pigeons, and smoke signals. On both land and sea the Knights were formidable warriors, undaunted in their defence of the Cross. In 1444—aided by 5,000 Rhodian supporters—they resisted attack by the Sultan of Egypt. Thirty-six years later they brilliantly outmanoeuvred the forces of Muhammad II, the Conqueror.

Under the Ottomans

In 1522, Suleiman the Magnificent moved against Rhodes. Infuriated that the Knights tolerated marauding pirates from Spain and Malta, yet intercepted and looted Turkish trading ships, he decided to get rid of the Christian bastion once and for all. On 24 June his massive force landed close to Iályssos. Shuttling back and forth from the mainland, 200 ships carried 150,000 soldiers, equipment, food, and supplies to lay siege to Rhodes. The Knights were now on their own. Europe lamented their plight—but ignored their distress calls.

In four and a half months, Suleiman lost 50,000 men in attempting to take the fortified city. The Turks were on the verge of giving up when a traitor, Amaral, revealed that the Christians were at the end of their tether. Suleiman decided to go all out and breached the walls. The Rhodians, facing famine, called for a truce.

So it was that on 1 January 1523—after 145 days of siege —the 180 Knights still remaining were allowed to leave honourably for Malta. They took with them 8,000 Christians, church banners, a variety of art treasures, and relics. Changing their name to the Knights of Malta, they stayed until Napoleon drove them to St. Petersburg, then to Italy, ending up with "branches" of charitable, unbelligerent associations in Britain and the United States.

For nearly four centuries, until 1912, Rhodes remained a minor Turkish possession. The four hundred years of occupation left an indelible imprint on the Rhodians, but Ottoman rule, both on Rhodes and elsewhere in the Mediterranean, was sleepy and decadent.

The Turks built—and destroyed—little, with the occasional church converted into a mosque by the addition of a minaret. The Grand Masters' Palace became a cattle barn, and once-noble inns were converted to barracks, with rickety wooden extensions. According to accounts by French writer Charles Cottu, the Turk "was content to squat on his carpet, puffing on his pipe throughout the centuries." Rhodes' forests were severely depleted.

Only Turks and Jews were allowed to live in the walled city; every night at the curfew bell, the Greeks working

Oh Deer

Deer have long been a feature of Rhodes, introduced during ancient times (prompted by the Delphic oracle) to combat the island's snakes, which were said to be repelled by their odour. In the modern era, the deer died out, but the island was re-stocked by the Italians, who had read their classics. Snakes are notoriously irreligious, however, and still hang around the island.

there had to leave for their homes in outlying villages. Offenders were beheaded. A new city, Neá Chóra (now Neochori), was established outside and around the city walls. In fact, the division of the two cultures ensured that traditional Greek customs survived, and even prospered. Linked closely to Greece through the Orthodox Church, Rhodes stayed very firmly Greek.

In 1821, mainland Greece revolted against the Turks and eventually won independence. Rhodes, too, tried to throw off its yoke but failed, suffering brutally as the Turks quashed the revolt. Not until the years before and after World War I was the Ottoman Empire at last dismantled.

Italy scored the first victory against the Turks and, with the Treaty of Lausanne in 1912, took over the Dodecanese islands—ostensibly in trust for eventual union with Greece.

A Place in the Sun

Unlike the Turks during their period of domination, the Italians immediately set to work excavating and restoring Classical sites and constructing roads, homes,

After liberation in 1945, a bronze doe replaced the Italian she-wolf at Mandráki Harbour.

and public buildings. They removed all Turkish appendages from buildings in the Knights' Quarter, and restored—after a fashion—the Palace of the Grand Masters as a summer residence for both Mussolini and Victor Emmanuel III, though the king was overthrown before he could ever use it. Much was destroyed in their zeal, but the Italians did develop an efficient irrigation system, as well as drenching the island in bougainvillaea.

Although the Rhodians suffered hardship under the occupation, the Italians made Rhodes a far more accessible island, and were responsible for the beginning of its development as a tourist destination.

However, it became increasingly clear that Italy had no intention of returning the Dodecanese islands to Greece, as had been the promise. In the late 1930s, the Greek language and Greek Orthodox Church were officially outlawed, and new plans were subsequently developed for turning the island into a summer retreat for Italian rulers.

Thus, the Dodecanese islands were to crown the Italian claim of *mare nostrum* in the Mediterranean.

After the Mussolini government fell in 1943, German troops landed on Rhodes and took over all Italian defence positions and military bases. The islands were finally liberated by British forces in 1945 and, after temporary United Nations trusteeship, were united with Greece two years later. Rhodes gained duty-free status, and Greece made plans to develop the tourist industry. Hotels were built, and facilities expanded.

Today they are still expanding, and Rhodes still succumbs to almost year-round foreign invasion. The cobbled streets of the Old Town again babble with many tongues, but these invaders are welcome, bringing with them a certain prosperity and stability. They come simply to enjoy the island's architectural heritage, and to worship Helios, the sun.

WHERE TO GO

From Rhodes Town at the northern tip, to the flower-covered hills of the interior and the quiet beaches of the south, Rhodes has something to please everyone. And when you know the island by heart, you can always take a boat trip to other islands.

Rhodes Town is made for walking, and besides, vehicular access to the ramparts is severely restricted. For visiting the rest of the island, it's a good idea to rent a car (four-wheel drive is the best for those unsurfaced roads in the south) or, even more popular here, a motorcycle or moped. Make sure you have enough fuel for your journey — in the south, petrol (gasoline) pumps are few and far between — and do not attempt to visit the whole of the island in one day by motorbike: the distances may look short on a map, but the roads are twisting and potholed, and those euphemistically marked as "unsurfaced" are, in reality, little more than dirt tracks. You can also take island buses to the most important sites, but make sure there is a return on the same day (return times as well as departures are given on timetables).

> **Signs:** ΑΦΙΞΗ – **Arrival** ΑΝΑΧΩΡΗΣΗ – **Departure**

RHODES TOWN

The capital is made up of two towns, the Old and the New. Whereas the New Town, with the exception of the harbour area, is without great charm, the Old Town, behind the fortifications, is the island's heart, in all senses. Wherever you're staying in Rhodes, you'll just about always find your feet taking you back here, through the ramparts into the narrow cobbled streets.

Just outside the walls, between Mandráki and Emborió harbours, lies **Platía Rimini** (Rimini Square), the hub of the two towns. Here you'll find the bus terminus, taxi stand, a place to deposit luggage, the New Market, Sound and Light Show, the entrance to the Municipal Gardens, and clean toilets, presided over by an old lady in black. Here also is the City of Rhodes Tourist Information Office. This should be your first stop, to check up on things that tend to change without notice, like museum opening hours, entrance fees, temporary exhibitions, and, of course, bus timetables.

The Old Town

Everyone makes a beeline for the old city, a maze of winding streets where, in spite of the crowds, it's always possible to escape and find a quiet corner of authenticity and calm. It divides neatly into two main areas: the Knights' Quarter, or

Textures of an age-old city can be seen at the Hippokratous Square Fountain in the Old Town of Rhodes.

Collachium, with its medieval monuments, and the Bourg, including the Turkish quarter, with bazaar and mosques, and the old Jewish enclave.

The Knights' Quarter

A good entrance to the Old Town is through **Píli Eleftherías** (Freedom Gate), so named by the Italians who saw themselves as liberators of the island from Turkish oppression. The name remained valid for the Greeks when they took over after World War II. The **moat**, which is between inner and outer walls and planted with bougainvillaea and rosebushes, never contained water; it simply discouraged invaders from putting up siege towers. As you cross over it, see on the left-hand side a little enclosure for a flock of deer, the symbol of Rhodes.

In the centre of **Platía Símis** (Symi Square), just inside the gate, are some of the rare vestiges of the ancient Greek city, column shafts and entablature fragments from the **Temple of Aphrodite**, third century B.C. A good view of the temple is afforded if you take the stairs over the Ionian and Popular Bank on the right-hand side to the **Municipal Art Gallery** (*pinakothíki*), which houses a small display of modern paintings by local artists.

Straight ahead lies **Platía Argirokástrou**. The fountain of marble in the centre of this square is a Byzantine baptismal font, discovered by Italian archaeologists in a church near

A Parade of Grand Masters

All over the Old Town, sculpted in stone on buildings, gates, and ramparts, the Grand Masters left to posterity their coats of arms. As you walk around, have a go at spotting who built what. You'll generally see two shields—the arms of the order next to those of the knight.

Arnitha in the south of the island. Behind it stands the 14th-century **Armeria**, or armoury, thought to have been the knights' original hospital. It is now the Greek Archaeological Service headquarters, its double staircase and doorway framed by a majestic purple splash of bougainvillaea. On the right-hand side of the façade is the coat of arms of Grand Master Roger de Pins (1355–1365). Note the cannonballs, heaped in neat pyramids. You'll see them all over the old town, by flowerbeds, used as football goalposts, or simply lying around. The iron ones were used by the Turks, while those of marble and limestone, more handsome but not so deadly, were fired in an earlier epoch.

The wing of the armoury building houses the **Museum of Decorative Arts**, a collection of folk art from Rhodes and other Dodecanese islands. If you're interested in buying authentic local handicrafts, it's a good idea to look here first for ideas among the embroidery, woodcarvings, and ceramics. A reconstruction of the interior of a traditional Rhodian home shows items in their proper setting.

Behind the Temple of Aphrodite is the **Inn of Auvergne** (1507), also with a fine Gothic doorway and an outside staircase leading to a gallery. Like many of the inns, it is now an administrative office. Pass beneath its archway, spanning the street, to the church of the **Panagía tou Kástrou** (Virgin of the Fort), which was originally the knights' cathedral. Its steeple was transformed into a minaret when it became the Turkish Mosque of Enderum (which Rhodians know as the Red Mosque, because of the Christians executed here). It now makes a lofty and imposing setting for the **Byzantine Museum**, which houses 14th-century frescoes, 15th-century icons from churches on both Rhodes and other islands of the Dodecanese, and a beautifully illuminated New Testament from Líndos, dating from the 13th century. The only reminder of its mosque days is the little fountain in the wall outside, beneath the plane tree.

Bypass for the moment the entrance to the famous Street of the Knights, to visit the august **Knights' Hospital**, the noble pretext for the island's massive defences and, indeed, the order's *raison d'être*. The chapel was above the grand Gothic doorway of the main entrance, where there is a bas-relief of two angels bearing the coat of arms of the Order of St. John. Beneath the angels, a marble scroll tells us in Latin that 10,000 florins were bequeathed by Grand Master Fluvian to build this inn.

His successor, Jean de Lastic, began building it in 1440 on top of Roman ruins, and it was completed under d'Aubusson. On each side of the main door, three arches cover storerooms now used by local merchants. The door leads into a courtyard, which, just beyond a faded mosaic floor from Kárpathos, is stonily surveyed by a lion of the first century A.D. retrieved from Rhodes necropolis. . The larger cannonballs scattered on the ground were probably catapulted over by Demetrius in 305 B.C. (see page 19).

The infirmary along the upstairs gallery held canopied beds and isolation cells for 100 patients. Surgeons tended pilgrims, often quarantined from recurring plagues. In a bizarre vicious circle, though, most of the patients were the knights themselves, wounded defending the hospital. They, in turn, had to make space for companions who continued the battle. . .and so on.

The hospital has been converted into the **Archaeological Museum**. As well as grand tombstones sculpted with the arms of the knights, and Grand Master Pierre de Comeillian's big marble sarcophagus, it has a fine collection of Mycenaean vases and jewellery as well as ancient sculpture. The life-sized, white-marble *Aphrodite* of the third century B.C., known popularly as the Marine Venus on which Lawrence Durrell wrote his *Reflections*, was netted off the coast of Rhodes by fishermen in 1929. An earlier and smaller *Aphrodite* (first century B.C.), more graceful, holds out her long wavy hair to dry in the sun after emerging from the sea. She was unearthed in Rhodes Town in 1912. Among the other sculptures are a small head of Zeus, found on Mount Attáviros; a life-like head of an athlete, probably a boxer; a 1.8-metre- (6-foot-) long grave slab (fifth century B.C.) from Kámiros, depicting in bas-relief daughter Krito bidding farewell to her mother, Timarista; and a striking head of the island's sun god, Helios (second century B.C.). Note the row of holes around his crown, designed to hold wire "rays." He was found near the Inn of Provence, not far from the spot where his temple is believed to have stood.

By now you must be ready to rest your feet. On the first floor of the museum is a charming little **garden**, cluttered with an eclectic mixture of stone and marble oddments, such as a dolphin and its baby, legless lions, bits of columns and old cannonballs, and headless statues, along with potted plants and shady trees, making it a perfect place to pause for reflection. Scattered here and there are little stone boxes with curved lids, made to hold the bones of ancient citizens.

On the other side of **Platía Moussíou** (Museum Square) stands the **Inn of England**, reduced to rubble by earthquake and an 1856 gunpowder explosion, and restored a century later by the British. In 1533, however, three years after their fellow knights had found a new home on Malta, the English left the Order following the pope's excommunication of Henry VIII.

 Now stroll up the narrow, cobblestoned **Odós Ippotón** (Street of the Knights), one of Europe's most remarkable medieval thoroughfares, thanks to meticulous restoration by the Italians, completed in 1916. (Come back after dark to see it empty and ghostly, and imagine scarlet-cloaked knights patrolling the street, their dim lanterns casting eerie shadows on the massive stone walls, the silence broken only by the echoing clatter of horseshoes on the cobblestones.) You'll come first to the **Inn of Italy**, on the right, facing the Knights' Hospital. Over the doorway is the emblem of 16th-century Grand Master Fabrizio del Carretto. Next door, the small **Palace of Villiers de l'Isle-Adam** honours Carretto's French successor, who had the unfortunate task of surrendering to Sultan Suleiman in 1522 (see page 25).

Opposite this mansion, the hospital's main gate led to the infirmary. A little farther on, behind a wrought-iron gate, is a charming shady **garden** with a Turkish fountain and the museum's marble relics stored among palm trees and shrubs. The

Odós Ippotón—an atmospheric street of medieval echoes, insignias, and hidden gardens.

A mixture of styles chronicles Rhodes' development at the Palace of the Grand Masters.

remains of a 15th-century building are probably from a Spanish inn, for the door is in Catalan or Aragonese style.

Facing the garden, with the royal fleur-de-lis amongst the coats of arms of Pierre d'Aubusson, Villiers de l'Isle-Adam, and Aimerie d'Amboise, are the splendid, late-Gothic façades of the **Inn of France**, with its **chapel** and **chaplain's residence**. Although the inscription on the doorway dates the inn from 1492, the chapel, with the Virgin and Child in a niche, bears the arms of an early grand master, Raymond Béranger (1365-1374). The inn's façade is worthy of more than just a passing glance, for it is the most beautiful and richly ornamented one of all.

Linked by the first of two arches which span the street, the simpler **Inn of Provence**, dated 1418, stands to the right, and the **Inn of Spain** to the left (split in two for the knights of Aragon and Castile). On each side of the Inn of Provence, a narrow cobbled alleyway leads to a garden behind a gate; if it's unlocked you can go in and look round. The Church of St. John, once on the left just beyond the street's second arch, was blown to smithereens by the gunpowder explosion of 1856, but part of the vaulted **loggia**, which originally connected the Palace of the Grand Masters and the church, has been restored.

When you reach the top of Ippotón, turn and look back to see the orderly sobriety of its perspective. The Italians did a marvellous job removing the colourful but clumsy clutter of ramshackle wooden balconies, added when the Turks billeted their troops in the inns.

The reconstruction of the **Palace of the Grand Masters** on Platía Kleovoúlou (Cleobulos Square) is more controversial. It may look better than the prison to which Suleiman reduced it before it was gutted by the great gunpowder explosion, but Greek scholars would have liked the ruins razed in order to dig for the ancient temple they believed to be underneath. As it was, Mussolini ordered the palace to be rebuilt in the 1930s as a summer residence, but World War II interrupted his holiday plans. What he left looks nothing like

Doctor Hippocrates

Local tradition claims that the great physician Hippocrates, who was born on Kos in 460 B.C., lived for at least 100 years. In fact, all we know for sure is that he was a contemporary of Socrates, active in the late fifth century B.C., that he was short in stature, travelled a lot, and died at Larissa on the Greek mainland. Of 72 works ascribed to him, only six seem genuine.

In his medical teaching, we know that he moved away from old magic towards more modern therapy based on empirical reasoning. He studied the effects of climate and environment on man's psyche and physiology, rejecting, for example, the "divine explanation of "the sacred disease" of epilepsy. His treatise on bone dislocation was still in use in the 19th century.

The famous Hippocratic Oath began: "I swear by Apollo the Physician and Asclepius god of healing to respect my teacher as I do my parents. . .not to give poison, though I be asked, nor procure abortion, to abstain from seducing male or female patients, and to observe professional secrecy."

the original medieval palace, but nonetheless presents a fascinating hodgepodge of Roman and Byzantine columns, floors paved with Roman and early Christian mosaics from Kos, and Italian Renaissance wood panelling. Invisible to the public eye are all the trappings of modernity—telephones, lifts, and central heating.

Take the monumental staircase to reach the rooms open to the public; they are grand and lofty, with huge chimneys in the corners, but sparsely furnished and gloomy. Some of the mosaics are delightful—note the Head of Medusa, the Nine Muses, the Dolphins, and Europa and the Bull. The best features of the rooms are the cool, marble window-seats and lovely views over the town and harbour. A small chapel with a Roman altar and some early Christian pieces are at the foot of the staircase.

Among the statuary in the marble-paved courtyard, note the bronze she-wolf, mother of Rome's Romulus and Remus, which originally guarded the entrance to Mandráki Harbour. Beneath the courtyard, storerooms (on three floors) were where the knights kept the cereals that saw them through Suleiman's siege, and reserves of munitions. Over at the far side, stairs lead down to an exhibition of Rhodian archaeological discoveries, including silver coins bearing the head of Helios, and particularly attractive, minute, heart-shaped glass beads in delicate colours.

On leaving the palace, note two marble inscriptions on the right, close to the courtyard entrance. In keeping with the symbolic "change of management" after World War II, one is dated "in the year of our Lord 1940, the 18th year of the Fascist era," while the other, from 1947, says it pays tribute to the "unconquered people of the Dodecanese" for preserving under "foreign occupation that inexhaustible fount of Greek civilization, the ideal of freedom."

As you leave Platía Kleo voúlou, turn right into **Orféos**, a street shaded by plane trees. Between St. Anthony's Gate and Amboise Gate, built by Grand Master d'Amboise in 1512, street painters have set up their easels; you can sit for a portrait beneath a row of cannons, muzzles aimed through loopholes in the palace wall above. Pass through **Amboise Gate** to get an idea of the fortifications surrounding the Old Town; the approach is via a stone bridge. Beyond its massive stone arch, cross onto a triple-arched bridge over an outer moat. Look back at the gate's imposing façade, further strengthened by squat round towers. Amboise Gate leads to the new part of Rhodes Town.

If you turn left on leaving Platía Kleovoúlou, you'll follow what was the south perimeter of the inner wall, which separated the knights' bastion from the remainder of the old town, and stretched from the clock tower to the harbour. Parts of this **Collachium wall** have been excavated, and you can see the ongoing digs behind wire fences on Panetíou, which is next to the Mosque of Suleiman, as well as farther down along Agissandrou.

The Bourg

During the time that Rhodes was held by the knights, the Greeks, Europeans, and Jews lived outside the Collachium wall, but still within the old city. Under Turkish rule, however, Greeks were obliged to leave the city confines by sunset. They have now taken their revenge by letting most of the mosques fall into decay. Although efforts are being made to restore them, progress is very slow, usually held up by interminable discussions about what kind of stone to use.

It's difficult to follow a map through these narrow, winding streets, where you are continually side-tracked by the mysteries of intriguing lanes and alleyways, and into courtyards paved with pebbles and covered in flowers. Tourists pack the main shopping streets near Sokrátous, where shopkeepers call out as you pass by: "Hello! Where do you come from? … Oh! My sister is married to someone from there …." Before you know it, you'll be invited inside and served coffee as if you were an old friend. You'll go in a shop by one door, leave by another, follow your nose through an archway, take a wrong turning—you're bound to get lost, but that's just part of the fun. There is no need to worry; the town is small, and if you wander too far off the beaten track, there'll be a handy orientation map to set you right.

At the top of Odós Sokrátous (Socrates Street) stands the **Mosque of Suleiman**, a landmark in patchy shades of terracotta pink. Until 1989 it had a lovely, double-balconied minaret, which made it stand out even more; unfortunately,

The Mosque of Suleiman provides a focal point for Rhodes' small Turkish community.

this started to lean and was considered a danger, so the authorities dismantled it. It now looks more like a disconsolate factory chimney and is awaiting restoration (but still features on all the postcards on sale). Built in honour of Sultan Suleiman after his conquest of 1522, the mosque was renovated 300 years later. Opposite, on the corner of Ippodámou, is the **Turkish Library** (1793), with an elegant inscription in Arabic calligraphy above the sculpted doors. Inside, two of the many valuable Arabic and Persian manuscripts are exquisitely illuminated Korans, both dating back to around the 15th or 16th centuries.

As you make your way down **Sokrátous**, you'll soon be immersed in the boisterous atmosphere of the old bazaar. Among the collection of ceramics, daggers, furs, jewellery, trays, pots, junk, and icons, you will find as many fakes as you could possibly imagine. About halfway down, a concrete leg sticking out into the road holds up the **Agha Mosque**, which was that of a Turkish Garrison Commander. A little fountain is set into the wall outside.

Walk under the mosque's arch into Odós Ag Fanouríou (St. Fanourios Street), then turn right into Menekléous, which winds into **Platía Aríonos**. Aríonos is a quiet square, with pleasant cafés and two big yellow buildings, both from 1765 and both bombed in World War II. One is the **Mosque of Sultan Moustafa**, closed and rotting—the faded green-and-ochre detail over the door also highlighted the pillars when they were standing. The other is the Turkish *hammam*, now restored to something similar to its old marble-floored splendour and serving the locals as the **Municipal Baths**. Why not drop in and steam away the worst aches of your sight- seeing muscles? It's perfectly clean, even if it might smell a bit dank. There is a modest entrance fee.

Between the two buildings, a lane leads to the Traditional Dance Centre (see page 80). Not far from this, next to a playground and again on Ag Fanouríou, is the ruined **Retjep Pasha Mosque**, once the most beautiful on Rhodes.

If you manage to find your way back to Sokrátous, head down to **Platía Ippokrátous** (Hippocrates Square) right at the bottom. In the centre is the **Sintrivani fountain**, with its little minaret topped by a dark green owl.

In the **Castellania** beyond, disputes were settled in the medieval courthouse upstairs, according to the legal code of the knights; downstairs was the stock exchange. Its flight of steps now serves as a grandstand resting place for footsore travellers; the sockets in the wall above their heads held banners to proclaim the court in session. This building was finished under the French Grand Master d'Amboise in 1507; the alligator gargoyles along the side are similar to those on the Inn of France (see page 36). Today the island's Folkloric Archives are housed on the top floor, while the public library is downstairs.

Behind this square, a short way along Pithagóra, you'll reach the **Mosque of Ibrahim Pasha** on Damagítou, in a relatively good state of repair. Born the illegitimate son of a Greek sailor, Ibrahim was sold into slavery and trained as a soldier and servant under the Ottoman Turks. He soon rose to high favour, wed the sultan's sister, and all but administered Suleiman's empire from 1523 to 1536. He was then strangled by order of the sultan. Built in 1531, the mosque was restored by the Italians, who added the new minaret.

If you have time to explore (you could spend hours here), continue going up Pithagóra and then stroll around the little back streets such as **Omírou**, **Ippodámou**, and **Irodótou**, all close to the walls. This area is quiet, and full of atmosphere and charm, retaining much of its medieval character.

Hippocrates Square and the Castellania — a popular gathering place, motorcycle park, and erstwhile stock exchange.

The archways were added by the Turks to consolidate the houses in case of earthquake, and in certain lights they form gloomy tunnels, enhancing the sense of age and mystery.

Keep looking up to catch all the fascinating architectural detail—a lattice window here, an Arabic inscription there, now and then a sun-splashed courtyard, an ancient fountain draped with washing, a beautifully carved door. You'll need to go up *and* down each street to discover all its secrets. Late at night these streets are a bit unsettling, however, and are best avoided by women on their own.

Otherwise, return to Platía Ippokrátous, then turn right on Aristotélous along the edge of what was formerly the old **Jewish quarter**. From the earliest days, the island's Jewish community played an important role in its commercial life. East of Pithagóra was notoriously noisier than the adjoining Turkish quarter.

Of the 6,000 Jews in the old town in the 1930s, two-thirds had emigrated by the outbreak of World War II. With German occupation in July 1943, the remaining 2,000 were assembled in what is now **Platía Evréon Martíron** (Square of the Jewish Martyrs), then deported to concentration camps. Only 50 survived. A handful of Jewish families remain on the island. The square is now peaceful, with the addition of a kitsch fountain with bronze seahorses. The lovely **synagogue**, indicated through an archway on Dosiádou next to a rusty plaque inscribed in Hebrew, is well worth a visit.

On the square behind the fountain is the **Episcopal Palace**, a potpourri of Gothic and Renaissance architecture. Before Suleiman's invasion, it was the residence of the archbishop of the Greek Orthodox Church. Today, souvenir shops have invested its arcades. Walk on towards the harbour gate; Alhadef Street cuts right through the ruined **Church of Our Lady of the Bourg**. Next to the Gothic apse, on the east, is a shady park with swings and slides, frequented by local children, their grannies, and a cock with his harem.

The Ramparts

For an overall view of the Old Town, it is a good idea to walk along the top of the ancient walls. The section open to the public covers about a third of the perimeter, from Amboise Gate to

Koskinoú Gate. Wear sensible shoes—sandals, slingbacks and thongs are not suitable—and don't go too near to the edge, which is not cordoned. A bronze plaque

Streets lined with colourful façades lead to an ancient synagogue in the Jewish Quarter.

by the gate warns you to keep hold of your children.

The fortifications are themselves a major work of military art, having evolved over the centuries as weapons progressed from arrow and spear to cannon and gunpowder. The walls grew increasingly massive, in places more than 12 metres (40 feet) thick, and were curved as well to deflect cannonballs. The southern section of ramparts—allotted to the English and Spanish knights—was particularly hard to defend, because the

Across the rooftops from the ramparts to the clock tower— a world invisible from the street.

land rises outside the walls, making them more vulnerable to attack. Here you can see extra towers and a double moat, and the fortifications are generally more extensive. Occasionally you'll notice an intricate carving of coats of arms.

Quite apart from the historical interest, the walk along the walls is attractive for the wild flowers and plants bordering the path and the lush vegetation in the moat. The Old Town looks amazingly green from up here—date palms and cypresses tower above roofs, dwarfing the minarets. You'll see a rooftop city quite unsuspected from street level: children playing among crumbling chimneys; mothers hanging up washing in the shell of a once-grand building; mossy slates; solar panels; a row of amphora lined against a wall; pots of scarlet flowers; a sunny marble terrace; cats on the prowl .... When you approach the end of the walk, look back to see all the stages in the old city's history spread out before you: the jumble of houses in the Turkish and Jewish quarters, peeling mosques and dilapidated minarets, the red-tiled dome of a Byzantine church, and on the horizon the stark silhouette of the Palace of the Grand Masters. The New Town is completely hidden from view.

The New Town

Under Turkish rule, the Greeks had to move outside the walled city and set up what came to be called Néa Chóra, the New Town. The area was first settled in ancient times, and construction work today continues to unearth remains of old civilizations. The commercial section in the northern part of the city, with its hotels, shops, administrative banks, cafés, and restaurants, is under 100 years old. Here, at night, the air reverberates with the insistent beat of disco music.

Start from Rimini Square and cross over into the **Néa Agorá** (New Market), a seven-sided, Oriental-style building. Its arcades surround an inner courtyard with stands of fresh fruit, meat, fish, and vegetables, and with souvenir shops. The cafés and restaurants are good vantage points from which to watch the action.

The New Market looks out to **Mandráki Harbour**, where the knights moored their galleys and modern tour operators dock excursion boats. The harbour's name is derived from its shape—"Mandráki" means "sheepfold"—but its entrance is guarded by bronze statues of a stag and doe. The doe, on the harbour's seaward arm, has replaced the she-wolf that symbolized Italian rule, which is now in the courtyard of the Grand Masters' Palace (see page 37).

The three **windmills** were built during the Middle Ages to mill grain for the departing cargo boats. Sea breezes still turn their jib-like sails, but the millstones came to a halt long ago. An earthquake destroyed another 14 windmills, which were lined along the breakwater of Emborió, the commercial harbour. Partly enclosed by the outer walls of the Old Town, this is used by larger ships and ferries. In the days of the knights, the harbours handled perfume and spices, oil, caviar, wax, wool, silk, sugar, wine, and slaves.

The town turns out for an evening stroll, the *vólta*, along the quays of Mandráki, where you can sign up for trips along the coast and to neighbouring islands, or sometimes to Marmaris in Turkey. Beneath notices describing the perils of their profession, sponge-divers show off their catch, and wizened old men sell dried fruit and nuts from little carts. On the other side of the road, beneath the arches of the New Market, friendly waiters try to lure you into their cafés with promises of iced drinks and calorie-crammed pastries. Go to the end of the pier for a view from the 15th-century **St. Nicholas Fort**, now a lighthouse with a chapel inside — Nicholas being the Orthodox patron saint of sailors.

Along the harbour, the dull administrative buildings — post office, harbour-master's office and courthouse — are

Schooners and yachts still anchor in Mandráki Harbour, but now the windmills turn in vain.

pompous contributions from the Italian régime. Opposite, and equally uninspired, is the Italians' effort to reproduce the **Church of St. John**, destroyed in the Old Town. It is the island's principal church, the seat of the archbishop of the Dodecanese. Beyond it lies the Governor's Palace, a pastiche of the Doge's Palace in Venice. The square facing the sea on the red-diamond-patterned side is named after Greek Admiral Periklís Ioannídis, who signed the agreement uniting the Dodecanese islands with Greece in 1947.

More ugly buildings—the national theatre and the town hall—are on the square named after George I of Greece, on the street side of the palace, sited on a busy, noisy corner.

North of the harbour, after the chic but private Nautical Club, lies the popular public **beach**, stretching around the tip of the island and down the western (windier) shore. The Elli Beach Club offers changing facilities, for a modest fee, and the beach is well supplied with showers, loungers, parasols and refreshment stands. This is also the site where the famous statue of the Marine Venus, which is now on view in the Archaeological Museum (see page 33), was dredged up.

Inland from the beach club, a graceful white minaret pinpoints the **Mosque of Murad Reis** and the **Turkish cemetery**. The Turks' chief buccaneer, Murad Reis, died in the victorious assault of

The sounds and smells of the New Market waft over the water; after shopping, go home by boat.

Epitaphs fit for a king — or at least a shah — adorn the tombstones at the Turkish cemetery.

1522 and is buried in a circular mausoleum next to the mosque. The entrance is through a shady, pebble-mosaic courtyard and, in spite of the main road beside it, the cemetery is a haven of peace—listen to the sickles of the fallen eucalyptus leaves crackle underfoot. Beautifully carved with flowing Arabic script and entwined leaves and flowers, the tombstones of the men are crowned by turbans or fezzes, while those of the women taper to a point. Ornate porticoes shelter the tombs of viziers, and even a shah of Persia, from sun and leaves, but, sadly, not from vandals, who have defaced several of them with red paint.

Standing alone at the tip of the island is the Hydrobiological Institute. In the **aquarium**, exotic sea creatures such as octopus, spotted morays and trigger fish swim around behind glass windows in tanks built and designed to resemble their natural environment. There is also a small museum, with a display of stuffed fish and various freaks of nature. It's good entertainment for the children on a rainy day.

Most of the buildings at this end of town are large hotels. Take the central avenue running through **Platía V Pavlou**, which is known to most residents as "100 Palms Square." Here you enter a district replete with British and Scandinavian cafés, bars, restaurants, and pubs, where only the occasional tiny Greek house has survived the foreign onslaught. Old ladies dressed in black sit on stools outside their doors surrounded by rusting olive oil tins and plastic dustbins filled with hibiscus, amaryllis, and honeysuckle, lost in contemplation of the colourful, rowdy street scene before them.

Follow Dragoumi or Griva down through a quiet residential area, where many of the doors bear plaques proclaiming them as doctor's surgeries, then turn left into any main street, which will bring you to the heart of the bustling "100 Shops District" around **Platía Kyprou** (Cyprus Square). You are now in what is definitely designer-label territory, with Italian names predominating. Farther along, Diakou and Papágou both resound with noisy bars, nightclubs, and discos where the young (and young-at-heart) very clearly have a great time, testing their stamina way into the early hours. A few yards more returns you to Rimini Square.

> Items marked ΕΚΠΤΩΣΕΙΣ are on sale.

THE OUTSKIRTS

Escape the crowds by taking a leisurely walk to the acropolis on Monte Smith, or cool and shady Rodíni Park. (Scholars can't agree on which was the site of the renowned School of Rhetoric.) Also within easy reach (a short bus ride away) is the delightful spa of Kallithéa.

Monte Smith

On the west side of town, the hill from where British Admiral Sydney Smith monitored the movements of the Napoleonic fleet makes a pleasant excursion at the end of the day. Either take bus number 5, or walk straight along Diagoridón

Rejuvenating waters at Kallithéa Spa; the Temple of Apollo (inset).

—it will take an hour from the centre of town at a very slow dawdle. The view of the Turkish coast and the islands of Tílos and Symi in the late afternoon sun is delightful. As the sun sinks, watch the ships from all directions homing in on Mandráki and Emborió harbours.

Amid olive groves, clumps of fragrant herbs, giant agaves, and prickly pears, the hilltop acropolis is crowned by the Doric **Temple of Apollo**. It was destroyed by the same earthquake that claimed the Colossus (see page 20), and Italian archaeologists have somewhat haphazardly resurrected three columns. They still serve as a landmark to passing ships, as they did in ancient times. Below the temple is the rebuilt **theatre** (where only the three bottom rows of dazzling marble seats are third-century originals), adjacent to the restored **stadium**, popular as ever with joggers and exercise fanatics.

Rodíni Park

This beautifully wooded park on the southern outskirts was landscaped by the Italians. It can be reached by taking city bus number 3, or by a (rather dull) walk of 3 km (2 miles) along Lindou. At the bottom of a ravine, a stream meanders between oleander bushes and cypress, plane, and maple trees. Follow the ravine path and you will reach a **Hellenistic tomb** with Doric half-columns, all carved from a rock outcrop. It's signposted as the Tomb of the Ptolemies, but it's unlikely that Ptolemies were actually buried on Rhodes. At the park entrance are a restaurant and nightclub; inside the park, peacocks strut disdainfully around heron, deer, rabbits, and chickens behind wire netting.

Kallithéa Spa

Under 10 km (6 miles) south of the capital, the peaceful spa of Kallithéa (*Thermes Kallitheas*) offers a bay with excellent swimming and scuba-diving and a small, sandy beach. (The bus from Rhodes Town leaves every half hour, the journey takes about 20 minutes; make sure you get the bus to the spa, and not to Kalithies, which is an inland village.)

The Italians tried to promote Kallithéa for the treatment of rheumatism, kidney and liver ailments, gout, and diabetes, building a beautiful, Oriental-style resort with domed pavilions and arbours shaded by palm trees. However, even the claim that Hippocrates, father of all physicians, came from Kos (see page 73) to take the waters failed to draw the crowds, and the buildings fell into disrepair.

Now the plaster and paint are chipped and peeling; birds dart through the broken blue panes of the star-shaped skylights to their nests above the windows. There are no changing facilities and the toilets must be the island's smelliest. What a wonderful place this would be if it were renovated—although then it would probably get overcrowded and you'd have to pay to get in. Be sure to bring your bathing equipment, as no one can resist the crystal clear water. Remember, also, plastic sandals—the sea bottom is covered in stones and prickly coral. A tiny shop sells sun-tan oil, cold drinks, ice cream, and postcards; behind the little harbour, a café in a hollow gouged out of the cliff serves all kinds of drinks, sandwiches, pizzas, and salads.

THE EAST COAST

Sheltered from blustery winds, the east coast offers pleasant excursions among beach resorts and orchards. A high point is Líndos (see page 55), historic trading port of ancient Greece and still one of the most beautiful villages in the Aegean, with the bonus of a splendid beach in its bay.

The first village you come to, about 6 km (4 miles) south of Rhodes, is **Asgouroú**. This was once a Turkish town, and there are still signs of Turkish influence in the architecture, but the village has developed into an industrial area. A few miles farther on at the hilltop village of **Koskinoú** you'll see the red-tiled roofs of the pastel, Neo-Classical houses. It's worth making a stop here to admire—from outside—these well-kept buildings, which are entered by an ornate portal in the wall of a pebble-mosaic (*chochláki*) courtyard. The living quarters for a whole family consist of a large room divided by a wide stone arch.

Farther along the main road, a turn-off leads to **Faliráki**, a booming resort with a long, crowded, sandy beach. A few miles farther is Rhodes' only golf course (18-hole), which overlooks the Bay of Afántou.

The main road sweeps past the suitably-named village of **Afántou**—the word means "invisible." Its hidden position kept it safe from both marauding pirates and Turks. A long

The interesting and colourful Archángelos cemetery is filled with decorated tombstones.

stretch of orchards starts here; the villagers make their living from apricots and weaving.

Modern hotel development hems in **Kolímbia**, which features a long boulevard shaded by eucalyptus trees leading to the sandy beach. The artificial waterfall pouring down by the side of the main road is part of the irrigation system the Italians built in the 1930s. A detour inland will take you to **Epta Piges** (Seven Springs), the source of the waterfall. To reach the man-made lake fed by the seven springs, you have the choice of either negotiating the rugged path or splashing through the gloomy tunnel of icy water. At the end there's a restaurant, shaded by pines.

Another turn-off on the coast road leads to the relatively quiet beach at **Tsambíka**. Stretch your legs with the climb to the town's white, hilltop monastery, from where there is a fine view to Rhodes' highest peak, Mount Attáviros (1,215 metres/3,986 feet). Every year on 8 September, local women make a pilgrimage to the monastery to pray for fertility. If their prayers are successful, resulting daughters are called Tsambíka, while sons receive the name Tsambíkos.

Archángelos is situated at the heart of the fruit-growing country, amid scenic groves of oranges, lemons, figs, olives, and grape vines. Towering above the lush countryside is the crumbling ruin of a 15th-century fortress, which is one of the many defences built by the Knights of St. John along the length of the coast as defence against the Turks.

The town, reassuringly unspoilt by tourism, has achieved renown for its splendid leather boots, which are hand-made to above the knee, but worn Puss-in-Boots style, folded or rolled down to the ankle. There is no difference in fit between left and right foot. The peasants have worn these boots since ancient times, for they provide protection against snakes. If you have the time, it's easy to have some made to measure.

Continuing in the direction of Malóna, you'll notice olive groves dotted with cypresses down in the valley. In spring, wild flowers turn the rolling countryside into a riot of colour. Signposts indicate **Charáki**, a fishing village recently developed with hotels and lively tavernas; a steep climb above it looms the castle of Feraklós, in which the knights locked up prisoners of war, as well as their own miscreants.

The road divides just beyond Kálathos. To the right are the developing resorts of Lardos and Pefkos, and somnolent villages with good, uncrowded beaches. The road continues to Kataviá, the island's southernmost settlement. Take the left fork for Líndos. As you reach the top of the winding road, brace yourself for the wonderful vista of this ancient port, crowned by castle and acropolis above the amazing blue sea.

LÍNDOS

The population of Líndos, estimated at 17,000 in antiquity, has dwindled to 700. But it can look like 17,000 when the tour buses roll in. Most houses here lay in ruins in the early 1960s. Then Líndos was discovered by the hippies. After that golden era, the tour operators took over, refurbishing homes into holiday apartments.

The tyrant Cleobulos, one of the Seven Sages of Greece, along with Solon and Periander, ruled Líndos for 40 years in the sixth century B.C. He left to posterity the saying: "Nothing in excess." Cleobulos would be most dismayed to walk down the main street today, past the racks of tacky souvenirs and tasteless T-shirts overflowing from the "tourist shops," to be assailed by the aroma of fish fingers, hamburgers, and chips. But don't be put off; you can't come to Rhodes and miss Líndos. The golden rule is to get here early. It really is worth rising at dawn for a first view over the sweep of the bay, the dazzling white village hugging the hillside, and the dark silhouette of the castle above.

There's just one main street from the village square, following the contours of the hillside, rising to the **acropolis**. The route is clearly marked. You can hire a donkey to help you up the steepest part (the stables are at the entrance to the main street), but the going is not too stiff. Be sure to wear comfortable shoes, which are essential, as the ground at the top is strewn with gravel and broken rock. When you get to the top, don't be tempted to lean over the edge—it's a sheer and unprotected 122-metre (400-foot) drop to the sea below. Village women lay out their expensive "hand-made" lace and embroidery (authenticity not guaranteed) over the rocks at the side of the path, just before a soft-drinks stand, where the donkeys set down their load.

Through the entrance gate, there is a cypress-shaded, walled platform on which you can rest for a moment before tackling the staircase up to the fortress. Hewn out of the rock at the base of the stairs is a huge second-century B.C. **relief** of a Greek *trireme* and an *exedra*, or curved seat. Despite its size, you can almost miss the carving on a dull day, or when the sun is shining directly on it. The pedestal in front of the ship held a bronze statue of Agessandros, a priest of Poseidon honoured in 180 B.C. for his care of the people of Líndos.

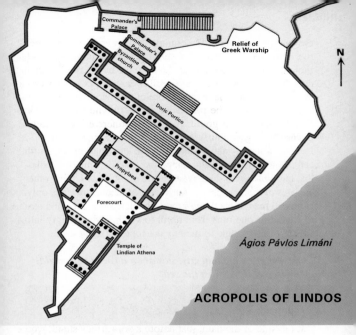

ACROPOLIS OF LINDOS

Climb to the **Commander's Palace**, which was first built in the Byzantine era and then reinforced by the Knights of St. John, and cross the vaulted hall, containing an assortment of both Classical and Hellenistic remains. You emerge into an untidy, stone-strewn courtyard. Turn left here and make your way carefully across the uneven floor of the dark chamber to reach the lowest terrace.

Adjacent to the palace are the ruins of the 13th-century Byzantine church of St. John, but this part of the acropolis is dominated by a wide, double-winged **Doric portico**, 87 metres (285 feet) long, which was constructed around 208 B.C.

Originally there were 42 columns; Italian architects restored the ones that are seen now. Behind the columns, a grand, monumental central staircase leads to the next terrace, which contains the foundations of the fifth-century B.C. *propylaea*, the entrance gate. From the bottom of this wide flight of steps you cannot imagine what lies ahead, for all you can see is the sky. As you mount them, the **Temple of Líndian Athena** comes into view. Fairly small—22 metres by 8 metres (72 feet by 26 feet)—and dating from the latter half of the fourth century B.C., it replaced a temple built at the time of Cleobulos, but which was destroyed by fire in 342 B.C. Unlike other temples of that day, its columns were at the narrow ends only, front and rear, and although most Greek temples are sited east to west, this one runs from north to south, fitting snugly into the apex of a triangle formed by the contours of the cliff.

Líndos, a great ancient city, stands on a rocky peninsula, gleaming white against the sea.

A goddess was worshipped on this rock long before the arrival of the Greeks. According to legend, the first sanctuary was erected by Danaus and his 50 daughters, the Danaïds, on their flight from Egypt to Argos, around 1500 B.C. This unnamed goddess would have been a matriarchal deity of the Middle Eastern religions, mistress of flora and fauna, and a protector of fertility.

Adopted by the Greeks as Athena of Líndos, or the Líndian Athena, she retained her pre-Hellenic nature. A temple was built to shelter her statue, which worshippers paid tribute to from afar, and to which they brought offerings such as fruit, sweetmeats, and drinks. No fire was permitted inside the edifice, and no oxen were sacrificed to the goddess, contrary to the usual custom in other Greek sanctuaries of Athena.

The first statue of Athena kept here was small and made of wood, depicting her seated on a throne with a crown and garlands of flowers. This was destroyed in the fire of 342 B.C., and replaced by a grander, upright statue, which was made of

It's All Greek to Me

Rhodes is so well geared to tourism that almost all notices and shop signs are written in English as well as Greek—and some only in English, such as "Super Market," "Tourist Shop," and "Foto Shop." Street and road signs are given in Greek, with an English transliteration. There is no hard-and-fast rule for spelling; Afántou, for example, can also appear as Afándou, because in certain cases the Greek *tau* is pronounced "d." Rhodes Town is always sign-posted "Rodos." The words for "street" *(odós)* and "square"*(platía)* are generally omitted from maps but appear on written addresses. Street names often appear translated into English; you can refer equally to Homer Street or Odós Omírou, Street of the Knights or Odós Ippotón (or Ippodón, of course). In general, we have given an English equivalent when an important street or square is first mentioned, and thereafter the Greek transcribed version.

gold, ivory, and marble. The new temple then became one of the Mediterranean's most important religious centres, attracting magnificent offerings thanks to the miracles attributed to the goddess. Now only empty pedestals and fragments of inscriptions remain.

If you look down from the walls, you can see the wide sweep of the northern harbour, busy with boats and water-skiers. At the end of the peninsula enclosing it is a large circular tomb, said to be that of Cleobulos, although there's no proof of this. To the south you can see **St. Paul's Bay**, seemingly enclosed by rocks when viewed from up here. St. Paul ended up on the island in a storm in A.D. 51, while sailing to Syria from Ephesus and Troy. There was a clap of thunder, the rock wall opened, and St. Paul's boat sailed to a safe anchorage. The spot where he landed is marked by a small white church.

Your tour of the village will take you through a maze of quiet lanes and alleyways, past little cubic dwellings and the Gothic-arched doorways and windows of beautifully refurbished 17th-century **patrician houses** in yellow sandstone, some now serving as pubs and restaurants. Peek in at the fine staircases and flowery, pebble-patterned courtyards. On top of some of the houses, arching over the roadway, are so-called "captain's rooms," with lookouts for passing ships. Below the acropolis at the southern end of the village, scooped out of the hillside, is the ancient **theatre**, with decorated gangway between banks of seats.

On your way back to the square, stop and have a look in at the 15th-century Byzantine **Panagía** (Church of St. Mary); you'll have probably noticed its bell tower and red-tiled domes from above. It was built by Grand Master d'Aubusson, between 1489 and 1490. In contrast with the simplicity of its exterior, the opulence displayed inside comes as a bit

The origins of Líndos were lost in mystery long before St. Paul arrived at this secluded bay.

of a shock. The floor is patterned with zigzags of black and white pebbles, and every inch of the walls and ceiling is covered with dark frescoes painted by Gregory of Symi in 1779. Ornate gold and silver icons and candelabra glitter in the uncertain light of beeswax candles, which fill the air with their heavy scent. Note in particular the icon of the Virgin, which is usually hung with votive offerings and has a jewelled tiara, and the beautifully carved bishop's chair.

THE WEST COAST

With fewer beaches on this windier side of the island, the most attractive excursions here are inland up into the hills. South of Rhodes, as far as Paradíssi and even beyond, most of the old villages are now engulfed by large, modern hotels. An exception is **Kritíka**, looking much as it did when settled by Turks fleeing Crete in 1898—a long row of identical houses like little boxes.

Ixía, the first resort out of town, is very lively, with a sparkling nightlife: the beach is popular with windsurfers. It blends into the ancient Minoan settlement of **Triánda**, now another booming resort. Above it on **Filérimos** plateau, only a few temple fragments and a fourth century B.C. Doric fountain remain from the great trading city of **Iályssos**. The Knights of St. John exploited its strategic position above the coast to launch their assault on Rhodes in 1309, before coming up with an offer the Genoese pirates could not refuse (see page 24). Also from the same point, Suleiman the Magnificent surveyed the last stages of his siege in 1522 (see page 25).

The 14th-century **Church of Our Lady of Filérimos**, built on the site of an ancient temple dedicated to Zeus, has been restored many times. The Turks stabled their horses in

The monastery at Filérimos.

it, and it was destroyed by bombs in World War II. Behind the church, the monastery cloisters are beautifully set among cypresses, and invite a peaceful moment of reflection. The monks' cells are identified by tiled plaques, each one depicting a different flower. Don't forget to visit the underground, barrel-vaulted **Chapel of St. George**, with its interior walls covered with restored 14th- and 15th-century frescoes illustrating scenes from the life of Christ. There is also an early Christian cross near the rear, carved in the stone wall, which was discovered under the plaster base of a section of fresco. Two other sites worth visiting on the hill are an 11th-century **Byzantine church** and the **Stations of the Cross**, the latter built by the Italians.

Continuing along the coast road through **Kremastí**, notice the American-colonial style of the schoolhouse (opposite the Neo-Classical library), donated by emigrants who left the town for the United States. Pass the airport (but keep an eye open for the pastel-coloured, Neo-Classical houses, with verandahs and Corinthian columns) and turn inland to the **Valley of the Butterflies** (*Petaloúdes*), which is indicated simply as "Butterflies" on the municipal buses.

Do not imagine that the butterflies remotely resemble the exotic specimens shown under plastic in the souvenir shops, for they are, in fact, a species of moth, *Callimorpha quadripunctaria*. Thousands of them come to this wooded valley in June and stay until September, attracted by the storax trees' vanilla-scented resin, which is also used for incense. From a camouflage of dark brown to blend with the rocks or storax bark, they open out in flight to a flutter of black, brown, white, and red. They earn their name, *Quadrina*, from four spots and a Roman numeral IV on each wing. Please respect this fragile, nocturnal species; like any self-respecting Greek, they do not appreciate interruptions to their daytime siesta. To protect their declining numbers, clapping hands or blowing whistles to prompt them into flight is strictly forbidden.

On reaching Kalavárda, the road divides. If you are ready to leave behind the heat of the coastal plain, take the inland route up to the pine-shaded resort on **Mount Profítis Ilías**, 798 metres (2,617 feet). Its two mountain lodges, Swiss chalet-style, named Élafos (stag) and Elafína (doe), have been closed for a while, but there is some hope that they will soon start operating again—ask at the Tourist Information Office in Rhodes Town (see page 125).

If you keep going for a short way on the coast road, you will reach the turn-off to **Ancient Kámiros**. This, the third of the island's ancient city-states, was probably founded by

Over 25 centuries have passed since Kámiros thrived as a city of trade.

Cretans who fled their devastated home. It prospered well into the classical era from eastern Mediterranean trade—and in apparent serenity, judging by the absence of any fortifications on the site excavated by the Italians in 1929. An even vaster city sleeps beneath the surrounding hills; the dig was interrupted by World War II.

The dramatic castle of Monólithos guards the island's southern tip, and offers Aegean views.

The bus from Rhodes sets down passengers at the bottom of a winding tree-shaded road; it takes about 20 minutes to walk up to the entrance to the site. In ancient times, statues placed among the trees welcomed visitors to the city. Just as you're wondering how much farther you'll have to walk, you blink, and there it is, a whole city, spread out in front of you in a hollow in the side of the hill.

Walk straight up the path to the tree-shaded ridge at the top, from where you can take in the whole settlement as it slopes gently towards the sea. You are now standing on the remains of a third-century B.C. Doric *stoa* (covered walkway), which stretches 195 metres (640 feet) from one side of the site to the other. Some columns were restored by the Italians, but they have since fallen down. The city's marketplace and religious and public buildings stood up here on the plateau.

Kámiros had a sophisticated water-supply system; beneath the *stoa* is a massive sixth-century B.C. cistern, which could hold 600 cubic metres of water; in Hellenistic times it was filled with earth, with the walkway built above it. You'll notice still-intact water pipes half-buried in the path.

Viewed from above, the residential area can be seen situated to the right of the main street running through the middle of town. A few re-erected pillars mark the site of a house of the Hellenistic period. Near the entrance is the sanctuary area, containing the remains of a Doric temple, with several columns in place. When you go down to look at it closely, you'll see footprints in the tops of many of the empty pedestals, the positions of long-lost statues, probably those looted by Cassius in 42 B.C. The walk back down to the bus stop is even more beautiful than that going up, as the sea forms an inky blue backdrop. There is a quiet little beach hidden away behind the tavernas.

Farther down the coast lies **Kámiros Skála**, with a modern fishing port which supplies some good, quayside seafood restaurants. It's the last stop along the sea before the road turns inland and into the mountains. From here caïques carry on trade with the isles of Alimniá and Chálki. If a hike and a picnic are more your style, turn west off the main road to the knights' 16th-century hillside fortress, **Kámiros Kastéllo**.

The main road loops round Mount Attáviros, the island's only real mountain. Nestling beneath its bald pate and surrounded by vineyards and tobacco fields is **Émbonas**, a village well-known for its women folk-dancers, who perform at festivals all over the island. Throughout the afternoon, you will see them intent on crocheting, sitting outside their front doors, while their men play backgammon in the tavernas.

When you wander past their houses the old women call out, inviting you to buy rag rugs or woven blankets displayed on the garden wall. Don't hesitate if you would like one: the rugs are extremely cheap and make lovely wall hangings and bedspreads. The women will happily show you their low, dark workrooms and huge looms.

Local honey and wine are sold in the village shops, and you can also visit the Emery and CAIR wineries (see page 98) for a free tasting.

Leaving Émbonas, the road twists and turns through lush and beautiful countryside, but is surfaced only as far as Ágios Issidorus. Just before you get to this village, there is a turn-off that leads across the island (a distance of 11 km/7 miles) to Laerma, but this road is also unsurfaced.

No need to hurry in Siána; seasons may come and go, but it seems that time stays the same.

From Laerma, you can drive to the tiny **Moní Tharri** monastery, built in the ninth to 13th centuries. There are up to four layers of frescoes on the walls inside, the earliest dating from 1000 A.D. If you want to visit the monastery, ask in Laerma for the caretaker.

Alternatively, pass through Ágios Issidorus and you'll find **Siána**, where time stands still—the hands of the church clock are painted on. The event of the day is the Monólithos bus executing a tricky manoeuvre in the middle of the village.

Monólithos (*mono* as in one, *lithos* as in rock) is the end of the line for west-coast buses from the capital. A 10-minute walk from the village brings you to a wooden bench, positioned for a glimpse of the 15th-century castle, balanced on the summit of the soaring monolith. The only sounds are the subtle rustle of dry fir cones in the breeze and the pounding of waves breaking against shingle 236 metres (774 feet) below. The road leads to the crumbling battlements. Inside are just two cisterns and a chapel, but the view alone, along the coast and to Chálki, makes the climb worthwhile.

The road to Kataviá from here is mostly unsurfaced. If you're the sort who likes going to the end of things, take the rough path from Ágios Pavlos to Cape Prassonísi, where a lonely lighthouse pinpoints the island's southern tip.

DODECANESE DAY TRIPS

At Mandráki Harbour, an array of ferries and caïques jostle for the honour of transporting you to Líndos or across to the outlying islands, while boats for Chálki depart from Kámiros Skála. In this section we include only those islands worth visiting on a day trip. Any farther afield, such as Pátmos and Kárpathos, take several days and can be reached by plane or boat. The place to find out about trips is the Tourist Informa-

tion Office (see page 125), or the travel agencies in town. To encourage tourism, there are sometimes free trips to Kastellórizo, far away near Kas on Turkey's Mediterranean coast. Keep a look-out for advertisements for such trips, displayed haphazardly around town.

Stop-off point for Panor-mítis monastery on Symi — a peaceful seaside retreat.

Chálki

This little snippet of an island, just 16 km (10 miles) west of Rhodes, is so peaceful largely because its sponge divers all emigrated to the United States to dive the waters of Florida's Tarpon Springs. Between them they earned enough money to pave Chálki's only real road, which runs from **Emborió**, the port, to the almost-abandoned hill town of **Chorio**, and is named Tarpon Springs Boulevard. The Neo-Classical houses of the harbour are being lovingly restored and repainted in ice-cream colours—vanilla, strawberry, and mocha—and above them all, the ruins of a crusaders' castle crown the hill. Tourism is limited due to an acute water shortage, for though some houses can store rainwater during winter, come summer the island relies on delivery of fresh water from Rhodes by boat.

The only beach worth mentioning is **Pontamo,** which is, in fact, one of the best sandy beaches in the entire Dodecanese group. All you need do here is laze in the sun, sample the excellent fish and lobster in one of the four tavernas, and relish your escape from the general hustle and bustle.

There are daily caïques to Chálki from Rhodes, leaving Kámiros Skála at 2:30 P.M. (or 3:00 P.M. Saturday) and returning at 5:30 A.M. (yes, that's 5:30 in the morning!). In addition, the weekly ferry from Rhodes to Kárpathos and Crete makes a stop at the island.

Symi

Boats to Symi leave Mandráki Harbour each morning at 9:00 A.M., usually calling in at Panormítis monastery, then hugging the barren, jagged coast up to Gialos, the harbour of Symi Town.

Up until the end of the 19th century, Symi was one of the richest islands in Greece, with the boat-building and sponge-

The port of Gialos on Symi has been described as the loveliest in Greece.

diving industries providing a livelihood for 20,000 people. After Italian occupation of the Dodecanese and World War II, however, the population dwindled to a mere 2,500. Today the islanders manage to earn a frugal living from sponge fishing and handicrafts.

As boats nose into Panormítis harbour, the bells of the **Monastery of the Archangel Michael** ring out in greeting. The beautiful **church** is laden with frescoes and icons. By far the grandest is that of Michael himself, portrayed as "captain of the heavenly host," clad in medieval armour and wielding a sword. In the small **museum** there is an exhibition of the church's treasures and ancient sponge-diving equipment. All the buildings lining the harbour belong to the monastery, including a restaurant and, in case you want to stay overnight, rooms with basic facilities. Here, as in all other Greek monasteries, women are only allowed through the door if dressed "decently"—no shorts or anything too revealing.

The approach to **Gialos**, at the end of a deep fjord, is delightful. Tier upon tier of elegant, pastel yellow-and-white, Neo-Classical houses rise up on all three sides, almost blending into the background. Only a few years ago, many of them were empty shells; now they have been converted into stylish hotels and apartments.

The harbour wakes up when the tour boats come in. You'll find restaurants and tavernas, craft shops, and stalls selling local products such as honey, herbs, spices, and essential oils. At the Sponge Centre you can learn all about the private life of a sponge, the best kind to buy, and how to look after it once you get it home. Swim at the little beach at Nos, to the north beyond the boatyard, or climb the 375 steps up to the "high town," or **Chorio**, a maze of winding streets slumbering all day long in the sun.

For those who want to stay here overnight, or longer, there's plenty of accommodation in Symi Town or at nearby Pedi beach (taxis are available from the south side of Gialos Harbour). A hike across Symi to Panormítis will take around four hours.

Kos

Kos is greener than most of the Dodecanese. Its fishermen boast of the best catch in the Aegean, and it produces fine wines, delicious table grapes, and a famous lettuce. The local hot springs are strong in iron for all that ails you, heartily recommended by the island's ancient physician, Hippocrates. But Kos becomes saturated in high season, and the bodies sardined along the beaches, or pouring into and stumbling out of the harbour cafés, may not be your glass of lager. How to beat the crowds? Try coming on a Sunday, when the shops are closed, to poke around the ruins in peace. Or rent a bicycle and ride farther.

Hydrofoils leave Mandráki at 8:00 A.M. and 6:00 P.M., and take two hours. Once on Kos, call at the Tourist Office on the main harbour (also called Mandráki) to pick up a free map; there's a lot to see, if you know the way.

A Skeleton in the Bathtub

The Ancient Greeks used sponges as paintbrushes, but no one realized that the sponge was an animal, and not a plant, until 1755. It lives up to 20 years, in colonies or isolation, fixed to a stone at the bottom of the sea, and grows in all shapes and sizes—bushes, fingers, cups, goblets, elephant's ears. Each sponge is a collection of cells, some of which lash little whips to create currents of water that bring food and oxygen. Others produce sperm and eggs, and still more build the skeleton. Protected from predators by its unpleasant taste and smell, the sponge has remarkable survival properties: the divers lop off the top, leaving a stump which regenerates. It has been discovered that if a sponge is ground up into minute pieces and pushed through a piece of muslin, it will reconstitute itself once returned to salt water. To reproduce, the sponge fertilizes itself, producing larvae or buds that break off and float away.

Overfishing resulted in depletion of sponges in the Aegean; now the sea is divided into five areas which are farmed in turn. When the sponges are harvested, the living, gelatinous cells are beaten out, and the remaining skeleton left to soak for a few days in the sea. Most are then bleached for exportation, but the experts will tell you that the unbleached variety—a rather unattractive dingy brown —lasts twice as long.

Looking down on Mandráki is the **Knights' Castle**, built in the 15th century with masonry from the Asclepium (see page 75). Its grounds are strewn with the flotsam of the island's ancient and medieval history—marble statuary and vases overgrown with wild flowers.

Behind the castle stands the 18th-century Mosque of the Loggia and, next to it, a huge hollow **plane tree**, branches propped up on crutches and in sore need of a tree doctor. It is very old, but not old enough to justify the claims that 2,500 years ago Hippocrates taught in its cool shade. The **fountain** unites life and death—its basin is an ancient sarcophagus.

Behind the mosque is the ancient **agorá** (marketplace), forming an integral part of Kos Town; people use its main street as a short cut between the harbour and the shops. The site is delightfully unkempt, as well as bewildering, since the remains date from a number of eras: Roman and Hellenistic temples, Byzantine churches, and part of a crusaders' bastion—all were revealed after an earthquake in 1933. Also near the mosque, six tapered, grey-green columns with elaborate Corinthian capitals can still be seen; they are what is left of a covered walkway dating from the fourth and third centuries B.C. which was later divided down the middle by a wall.

The **Old Town** is an area of little streets of whitewashed houses and craft shops, emblazoned by the pink and purple petals of wisteria and bougainvillaea. The colourful Turkish quarter is a reminder that half the town's population—close to 5,000—is Muslim. A sign secured to the old *hammam* invites you to go in and visit, but don't expect it to be too grand, since the restored bath-house is now home to a family's washing machine. In the back garden, however, a few tables are set beneath shady trees to make a peaceful and inexpensive restaurant.

Go down the steps beyond the *hammam* and you come to the L-shaped "**Western excavations**," including a stadium, early Christian basilica, acropolis, and about 145 metres (160 yards) of paved, die-straight Roman road, complete with cart ruts. The restored bath-house comprises a peristyle of beautiful Ionic columns around a marble paved courtyard; sneak a look in the window.

Sheltered by a wooden shed is a large mosaic floor; there are more mosaics around the site, some of which are protected beneath a layer of sand, others by sheds. The best examples of mosaics from Kos are in Rhodes, in the Grand Masters' Palace.

On the opposite side of the main road stands the Roman villa, **Casa Romana**, where a number of lovely mosaics have been restored, surrounded by blank walls and flat roof.

An ancient sarcophagus by Hippocrates' tree shows the past is never far away.

Continuing, follow the avenue of cypresses to discover the Hellenistic **theatre**, which is still used on occasion for Classical drama performances.

Back in town again, next to Deftedar Mosque on Kazouli Square, is the small **museum** which exhibits archaeological finds from the island. A courtyard reconstruction has been done with a mosaic floor, and many statues illustrate the connection with the medical world—for instance Hygeia, goddess of health, with assistant Hypnos (Sleep) at her feet, and a fourth-century A.D. representation of Hippocrates.

The **Asclepium**, a terraced sanctuary and medical school founded in the fourth century B.C. after the death of Hippocrates, is 4 km (2½ miles) out of town. At the lower level are remains of a Roman bath (first century A.D.), which exploited the iron- and sulphur-rich waters of the island. You will see some fine Ionian column capitals on the middle terrace, but the principal Doric Temple of Asclepius is on the upper terrace. From here you have a good view of the Turkish mainland, with the Knidos peninsula to the south and Bodrum (ancient Halicarnassus, home of historian Herodotus) to the north.

If you are staying on Kos a few days you might like to discover its **beaches** (the one in Kos Town itself is a rather disappointing strip of shingle by a main road). The most popular are along the north coast at **Tigaki** and the fishing village of **Mastichari**. The distinctive feature of **Ágios Fokas** on the southeast coast is its black sand. At the west end of the island, Club Med has planted flags on **Ágios Stefanos Bay**. Nearby, **Kefalos** offers good sandy beaches, lively tavernas, and a working flour mill.

Inland, high on the slopes of Mount Dikeos, **Asfendiou** is a charming commune of white stone houses, where the bread is baked in stone ovens in the courtyard among the fig trees.

WHAT TO DO

As soon as you get off the boat or plane into the sunny climate of Rhodes, you'll want to do as the Rhodians do, and spend all your time outdoors.

ENTERTAINMENT

It doesn't take much to keep the Greeks content. They are fond of simple pleasures—an evening stroll along the harbour, an hour or so in a café, sitting beneath the plane trees discussing politics or playing backgammon, a late meal in a taverna, rounded off by dancing and singing.

On the whole though, entertainment here is largely geared to the tourist industry. No one could complain that the island is quiet—the New Town glows with neon lights; the crowded and rowdy English and Scandinavian bars and pubs burst at the seams; the air throbs all night long to the beat of disco music. The resorts down the coast and at Líndos are just as lively as Rhodes Town, though it has to be said that the 3:00 A.M. streetlife is fun if you're in the mood, but tiring if you want a good night's sleep.

In the Old Town, the island villages, and dotted here and there among the high-rise concrete hotels, you'll still find tavernas with traditional food, music, and dancing. The music is plucked on a *bouzoúki*—a stringed, pear-shaped instrument similar to the mandolin. (Some say that it is not Greek, but Turkish in origin.) In many restaurants the *bouzoúki* music blares from a radio or scratchy record player. It doesn't really matter to the Greeks, so long as it's loud.

Authentic **Greek music** can trace its roots back as far as the eighth century B.C., when dancing was an essential part of pagan religious rites. The fluted pipe of Pan and Apollo's lyre are today's clarinet and *bouzoúki*, tempered by the chants of the Byzantine church. While the Ottomans ruled, Greek Orthodox chanters earned their living by singing Turkish songs in the houses and palaces of local pashas. Those 400 years of Turkish music, much influenced by the nasal intonation of Arab wailing, left its mark.

Due to the singing of Nana Mouskouri, the films of Melina Mercouri, and the compositions of Mikis Theodorakis, who wrote the music for *Zorba the Greek*, some Greek music is now known internationally. Theodorakis found the inspiration for his alternately harsh and plaintive popular music in the *rembétika*, a genre created by the militant urban youth of the tempestuous 1920s, after the mass exchange of Turkish and Greek populations. Their songs dealt with love, poverty, and parting from Greece, but today the lyrics are often based on themes from modern Greek poetry, inspired by the writings of such as George Seferis, winner of the Nobel Prize for Literature in 1963. After the Greek army coup in 1967, the songs were often about political suffering and loss of freedom. Protest songs by Mikis Theodorakis were banned during this period.

Folk dancing plays an integral role in Greek cultural life and makes a lively evening's entertainment.

FESTIVALS and HOLY DAYS

Celebrations of saint's days usually begin the evening before.

January 1: New Year's Day or St. Basil's Day (*Protochronía*). Card games begun the night before and finished on this day test the luck of the Rhodians for the coming year. You might be offered a sprig of basil as a symbol of hospitality.

January 6: Epiphany Day (*ton Theofaníon*), the day waters are blessed in all Greece. In Rhodes Town, a cross is tossed into the harbour and children and young men try to retrieve it from the chilly water. The one to surface with the cross is ducked, then anointed with oil, blessed, and given coins. White pigeons are released to fly overhead during the ceremony.

Greek Carnival: *Apókries*. For three weeks preceding Lent there are colourful processions and raucous parties, with the merrymakers donning costumes and masks.

Clean Monday: *Katharí Deftéra*, first day of Orthodox Lent. A day of fasting; some people eat only potatoes and garlic.

7 March: Union of the Dodecanese with Greece, celebrated by parades and folk dancing.

25 March: National holiday celebrating the 1821 revolution against the Turks.

Easter: *Páscha*. Solemn processions in towns and villages. The celebration of divine liturgy at midnight on Holy Saturday marks the beginning of Easter. When the priest proclaims *Christós Anésli* (Christ is risen) the church courtyard suddenly turns festive: church bells peal, fireworks are set off, each member of the congregation lights a taper from the priest's candle and tries to get it home without it going out—a promise of good luck for the following year. **Note** that Orthodox Easter does not always coincide with Easter elsewhere.

May 1: May Day (*Protomagía*). Young men hang wreaths and bouquets of flowers on their sweethearts' doors and cars; they stay there till the end of the month.

Pentecost: Festival at St. Michael's Monastery at Panormítis.

June 24: Birthday of St. John the Baptist: feasting, bonfires.

July 29 and **30**: St. Saul's Day (*tou Agíou Soúla*) held near Soroni with lively celebrations, including donkey racing. By some strange historical mix-up, St. Saul is identified with a companion of St. Paul when he was shipwrecked at Líndos.

August: Dance festivals in Maritsá, Kallithiés, and Émbonas.

August 15: Assumption Day (*tis Panagías*). The most renowned festival in the Dodecanese, with religious processions and dancing in Kremastí and Triánda.

September 8: Birth of St. Mary (*Génnisis tis Panagías*). At Tsambíka, on the eve of this holy day, women climb the steep hill in a procession to the monastery to pray for fertility.

October 26: Feast of St. Demetrios; the new wine is tasted.

October 28: "*Ochi*" ("No") Day, a national holiday.

November 30: St. Andrew's Day: everyone eats *loukoumades*—honey-drenched doughnuts.

December 24: Christmas Eve. Flat buns, or "Christ's Loaves," are baked.

Dancing has long been a criterion of masculine prowess and feminine grace. Traditionally, men danced in tavernas alone, while women danced in the village square in groups. When a Greek gets up to dance in a taverna, he's re-enacting his heritage and literally retracing the steps of his ancestors. He often acts on impulse, feeling a need to express joy, well-being, or sorrow.

The *zeybékiko*, originating from Asia Minor, is an introspective meditation dance, in which the man slowly sways, his eyes half-closed, arms outstretched, leaning backwards, occasionally taking a step forwards or sideways and making a sudden sharp twist or leap before adopting a more deliberate rhythm. This turns into the *khassápikos*, or butcher's dance, in which two or three men link arms and find a community of spirit by swaying, dipping, and stepping together, the sudden changes signalled by a shout or squeeze of the shoulder from the lead dancer carrying a handkerchief.

Other Greek dances are the *tsámikos*, which is a handkerchief dance, *naftikós*, a sailor's dance, and *michánikos* of Kálymnos, in which an old and crippled sponge diver valiantly attempts to skip around as he did in his youth. The *sirtáki*, which was popularized by Anthony Quinn's Zorba, is in fact a combination—invented for the film—of a variety of distinct traditional dances. Staged at resort tavernas and nightclubs, this is when the dancers smash plates or toss gardenias, according to temperament.

The best place to see folk dancing is at weddings, festivals, or the open-air theatre of the **Traditional Dance Centre** on Androníkou in Rhodes Old Town. Here, Nelly Dimoglou's cheerful troupe is dedicated to preserving the folk traditions of all Greece, and they perform dances from Macedonia, Epiros, Corfu, and Thrace, as well as the Dodecanese, ending up with a foot-tapping *sirtáki*. The centre also runs a workshop, in which craftsmen work on traditional costumes.

At the foot of the old walls, the balmy Municipal Gardens are a pleasant setting on warm summer nights for the **Sound and Light Show**. The performance (three times nightly in different languages) recounts the last hours of the heroic defence of the city against the siege of Suleiman the Magnificent (see page 25). The eerie atmosphere is spoiled only when the clash of swords is drowned by a plane overhead.

All year you can have a fling or a flutter in the **casino**, at the Astir Palace Grand Hotel. This was the brainchild of a group led by Baron von Richthofen, nephew of the World War I flying ace. In the early days, the croupiers were flown in from

Baden-Baden in Germany. Try your luck at blackjack, American roulette, and *chemin de fer*; there are also slot machines to swallow up your loose change. You'll need your passport to get in, and note that jeans are not allowed, and men have to wear a shirt with collar—although a tie is not obligatory.

There are several **cinemas** in Rhodes Town. Foreign films are shown in the original language, with Greek subtitles.

Check with your hotel, ask at Tourist Information, or listen to Radio 95.9 International (5:00–6:00 P.M.) for information about plays, folk dancing, or classical music concerts, which are usually at the **National Theatre** or **Medieval Moat Theatre**, both of which welcome international orchestras and ballet companies as well as famous Greek musicians. A night out at the theatre is a great event for Rhodians themselves, and it's worth joining the audience just to see everyone dressed up to the nines, the women and girls often glittering with gold and diamonds.

SHOPPING

Try on a fur coat, buy a carpet, order some carved chairs, have shoes or a suit tailored, splash out on Chanel(-type) perfume, or fall for a furry banana with a skin that unzips—Rhodes has shops to please everyone.

The New Town is crammed with a multitude of upmarket designer boutiques, as well as off-licences selling alcoholic drinks from all over the world, in a rainbow of colours and in every possible kind, from advocaat to *Zwetschgenwasser*. The bazaar atmosphere in the Old Town prevails, with goods spilling out into the street, the proprietors sitting outside trying to lure you into dens festooned with piles of sandals, plates, cheesecloth dresses, and woven blankets.

Rhodes was granted special low-duty privileges following the unification of the Dodecanese islands with Greece in

1947. As a result, foreign imports are cheaper here than in their country of origin—which explains why so many shops have flourished. On the other hand, goods which have been imported from Athens tend to be more expensive than on the mainland, because of shipping costs and local taxes. Prices are fixed in major shops and fashionable boutiques, and on most of the brand-name goods. There's more freedom to bargain in the smaller bazaar-type shops in the Old Town; generally, vendors will lower prices as soon as they see you dithering. Here it's certainly best to look round all the shops before you purchase anything—many offer similar goods but at very different prices. Quality varies, too, so don't hesitate to pick things up and examine them.

Most shops in Rhodes Town close from 1:00 P.M. to 5:00 P.M., during the siesta hours, but then stay open fairly late, until between 8:30 P.M. and 10:30 P.M. In villages, opening hours of shops and stalls with local products and handicrafts

Greek pottery makes a good souvenir — just check that it's not antique.

are determined by the arrival of the bus from Rhodes Town. Turn up in the early hours, and you'll find nothing but closed doors and silent, empty streets. One thing is sure: in the resorts visited by big-spending cruisers—like Rhodes and all the other Dodecanese—boutiques will remain open until the last passenger is back on board the ship.

If it's food you're after, try the Néa Agorá (New Market) across from Rimini Square in the New Town (see page 46). This has always been Rhodes' traditional market, though many stalls selling fresh fish, fruit, and vegetables have now been replaced by small cafés serving sandwiches and *souvlákia.*

Alternatively, seek out one of the public markets (*laiki*), which are now very popular. They are held every morning from Wednesday to Saturday in certain streets of the town. Local village people come to sell fresh fruit and vegetables, often at cheaper prices than in shops. *Laiki* begin early (6:00 A.M.), when prices may be somewhat inflated, but they have usually dropped by the time the stands are packed up around noon.

Best Buys

A large proportion of Rhodes Town shops sell the kitschiest of souvenir junk—*oúzo* bottled in Corinthian columns, plastic worry beads, and fluorescent T-shirts emblazoned with rude messages. Nonetheless, you can still find some good buys if you know where to look.

Antiques: If you buy genuine antiques, they must come with an export permit as well as the approval of the Archaeological Service and the Greek Ministry of Culture and Science, which is virtually impossible to obtain for anything truly ancient. Customs officials keep a keen eye open for big pieces, while small, easily smuggled items such as figurines are probably fake anyway (but don't hesitate to seek a second opinion if you believe you have something of genuine worth). Law-breakers face a stiff fine and a prison sentence of up to five years, so if you stumble upon an ancient amphora or Byzantine icon, make sure you have the appropriate export licence before trying to take it home. Check with the Archaeological Service, which is at Platía Argirokástrou; tel. (0241) 27674.

Those little marble chunks lying around the archaeological sites may look like the perfect paperweight, but don't be tempted to snaffle them; you'd be in serious trouble.

Byzantine icons are easily faked; best be content with a replica. Go to the showroom of TAP (Archaeological Receipts Fund) on the corner of Odós Ippotón, where you can order casts of exhibits from Greece's most famous museums. Each item includes a certificate of authenticity and export permit.

Brass and copperware: Have a look along Sokrátous in the few tiny shops which sell authentic, ancient, long-handled coffee pots, brass lamps, shelf brackets, and so on, retrieved from old Turkish homes. Also popular are long skewers for grilling your own souvlákia on the barbecue, and elegant brass coffee grinders engraved with the Rhodian flower pattern.

Carpets: A few shops along Sokrátous offer the chance to watch women knotting intricate patterns onto a loom, with nothing but their fingers, wool, and a sharp knife. The typical Rhodes model has the inevitable deer in the centre.

Deer but not always dear — carpets and embroidery often bear this traditional Greek motif.

Ceramics: World famous for its decorative beauty, Líndos pottery is cheerfully patterned with flowers, birds, and animals in bright primary colours. The plates are designed with two little holes in the back to insert a wire—look in the Museum of Decorative Arts (see page 32) at how they are hung on the walls of traditional homes. Their style is believed to be Persian in origin.

Unfortunately, most Líndos pottery in the shops is gilded with 18-carat gold, which multiplies the cost by at least four times. To find the real thing, go to Líndos, or visit one of the factories such as Ikaros on the way, and watch the painting in process. An unusual souvenir is a little tile with your house number, bordered with flowers or leaves; these are set into the walls of many houses in town.

You can also buy replicas of Minoan and Geometric vases, and pleasing modern, chunky pottery in every possible shade of Aegean blue.

Clothing: Top-quality fabrics—cashmere, camelhair, flannel, Harris tweed, worsteds—are available at close to duty-free prices, and snipped and sewn into made-to-measure suits by the town's many tailors. You'll find them in the New Town's "100 Shops" area. Reckon on three fittings (in three days).

On Rhodes fur coats are cheaper than in many places. Fox and mink can be imported without permits. Be warned that many furriers sell the

> **Sizes can vary. Be sure to try on clothing and shoes before you buy.**

skins of spotted cats—an illegal practice, no matter what the shopkeeper says. Trade in lynx, ocelot, wild cat, leopard, panther, jaguar, and cheetah is forbidden or strictly controlled by CITES regulations.

Food and drink: Prices for wine and spirits are lower on Rhodes than in the airport duty-free shops, and there is an immense variety; but look at the labels very carefully, and choose familiar brand names—some of those "genuine Scotch whiskies" are too Highland-laddie-sounding to be true.

Tins of local herbs, olives, olive oil, Greek Delight, honey and so on, are all considerably cheaper in supermarkets than at the airport.

Jewellery: In Greece, the styling of jewellery in silver and gold is dictated more by ancient history than any recent regional tradition. The jewellery designers have moved on from the time-honoured lacy silver filigree to draw inspiration from the country's great museum collections. It's not easy to improve on the elegant Byzantine style, or bracelets, earrings, necklaces, and rings of the ancient Minoan civilization. Equally as timeless are the ancient designs for plates, bowls, and chalices.

You will also find modern designs crafted with admirable workmanship, incorporating semiprecious stones imported from Italy into striking silver settings . When silver and gold (which are most often 18-carat) are sold, both are priced by weight, with a fraction of the cost added for workmanship and creativity. The Old Town is a great place for treasure-hunting—try not to miss the beautiful pebbled-paved show-room of Ilias Lalounis, which is on Platía Meg Alexandrou in the Knights' Quarter.

Leather goods: Leather shoes and sandals are good buys, as are the wide boots of Archángelos, which you can have made in the village itself or by cobblers in the back streets of the Old Town. The cowboy hats will last for ever, though they are a little heavy to wear as sunshades. Some of the handbags, rucksacks, briefcases, and larger pieces of luggage are extremely attractive and economical, but look carefully at seams and make sure buckles are firmly fixed before you buy anything.

Local handicrafts and produce: The following will make unusual souvenirs: woven blankets, rag rugs, wine, and runny, golden honey from Émbonas; natural sponges sold by the divers (or their wives) at Mandráki Harbour and Symi; pottery, silk-screen paintings, and batiks in Rhodes Old Town; herbs, spices, herbal teas and oils, attractive rustic pottery, and hand-painted sea-pebble miniatures on Symi; and hard-wearing leather boots from the town of Archángelos.

Woodcarving: Letter holders, trays, folding tables, walking sticks, key racks, and chairs, all carved with intricate flowers and leaves, and sometimes inlaid with brass or mother-of-pearl, are very attractive buys. Also popular are salad bowls, carving boards, bracelets, and mortars and pestles made from olive wood.

SPORT

The choice of recreational activities on Rhodes is excellent and diverse, ranging from hiking and karting to underwater swimming and snorkelling.

Watersports

Even though the local, unpredictable *méltemi* (north wind) can make **sailing** in smaller boats very tricky, you'll probably want to venture into the blue on a calm day. To rent a boat, just walk around Mandráki Harbour until you find one that suits you; the owner will be there, always ready to vaunt its merits.

At present cluttered with a chaos of day-trip boats, hydrofoils, yachts, pirate ships, sailing boats, caïques, and motorboats, Mandráki is scheduled to receive a new marina, which will eventually increase and—it is hoped—rationalize mooring space. You could also try the Rhodes Yachting Club at 9 Koundouriotou Square; tel. (0241) 23287 (near Elli Beach Club).

Two-seater **pedalos** are just the thing for a leisurely trip exploring harbours and coves. You'll find them available for hire on most beaches along the length of the east coast, where the sea is calmer.

Water-ski enthusiasts will also want to head for the east coast. Try Faliráki beach, Líndos, or several of the hotels. Prices vary according to location, size of boat, and length of time hired. **Parasailing**, **windsurfing,** and **aqua-scootering** are also very popular.

A fun sport for participants and watchers alike (although not great for the environment) is **ski-boating**, which is called here either "sausage" or even "banana" rides. You sit astride a bright, inflatable rubber raft towed behind a motorboat, and cling on for dear life while it speeds across the bay. Everyone ends up being thrown off into the water, amidst much shrieking, splashing, and frolicking—it's all as easy and natural as falling off a log.

The east and west coast of Rhodes both have a shingle **beach**. The west has the advantage of the setting sun, but in the morning is fairly chilly. Most people head for the east beach, between the Yacht Club and the Aquarium. Here there are fresh-water showers, and parallel rows of sun beds and parasols—to protect you from the breeze, not the sun. Several kiosks provide ice-cream and soft drinks. The sea in this area is superb for **swimming**.

Note that nude sun-bathing and swimming away from designated areas are both treated as punishable offences; there seem to be few objections to going topless however—just about everyone does it.

Faliráki beach is long and sandy, sloping gently out to the sea, and so is ideal for children. It is also the most popular beach on the island and consequently the most crowded. If a quieter setting sounds better, continue south and you will find a sheltered and often tranquil bay. Faliráki has plenty of seaside amenities, including changing cabins, restaurants with rooms to let, parasols, showers, and deck-chairs. During summer, a frequent bus service operates from Rhodes Town.

The tiny, secluded beach at Kallithéa Spa, where the sea is incredibly clear, remains relatively peaceful. If you want to find an isolated desert-island beach, however, you will have to go much farther south, to the long, smooth stretches of sand beyond Líndos.

Swimming on Rhodes' west coast is more hazardous, due to the wind and choppy seas. South of Kámiros, the coast is rocky and craggy, but the bay of Kámiros has an excellent beach, and you can swim here without risk if the sea is calm.

Before you zip yourself into a wet suit, take note that **skin divers** are not allowed to tamper with or remove archaeological remains from the sea bed. If you think you've spotted a relic, you're expected to report it to the authorities.

You don't need a permit for **spear fishing**, but you are not allowed within 90 metres (100 yards) of public beaches. Be sure when you spot a target that the fish weighs more than 150 grams (5 ounces). For the best fishing, explore the shores of Líndos, Kámiros, Kallithéa, and Genadi.

Pedal power — it's as easy as riding a bike and a fun way to find coves and caverns.

Snorkellers will find plenty of colourful fish swimming in the warm Aegean, and scores of hermit crabs scampering in amongst the rocks and pebbles on the sea floor.

Inland Sports

Rhodes has only one 18-hole, (par-73) **golf course**, which is at Afándou, around 22 km (14 miles) south of Rhodes Town; tel. (0241) 51256. Professional coaching is offered here and there are hotel and restaurant facilities available.

Speed enthusiasts can enjoy **karting** on the track near the military airport at Damatria.

Municipal **tennis courts** are located next to the Elli Beach Club. Many hotels also have courts open to the public, and equipment can be rented on the spot. Ask at your hotel if you can reserve a court nearby.

Joggers will appreciate the bracing air and open spaces up on Monte Smith. Join others in running round the stadium in the tracks of ancient athletes.

The most suitable place on Rhodes for **hiking** is on Mount Attáviros above Émbonas. The best idea is to ask the villagers for directions, since the mountain path is somewhat difficult to find. It takes roughly three hours for the full hike; and don't attempt it alone. At the top are a few scant remains of a Hellenistic temple to Zeus, and a wonderful view of the island. If you want to stay in the area overnight, accommodation can be arranged in private rooms in the village.

When it comes to **football**, two of the island's teams play in the Greek national football league 3rd division: *Rodos* and *Diagoras*. Rhodes itself supports three local divisions, and the top teams have play-offs with other regional winners for a position in the national 3rd division. Regular matches take place in the stadium just behind St. John's Gate in the New Town most Sunday afternoons.

EATING OUT

The basic dishes at a Greek meal have not changed much since Plato's Banquet. Lamb, goat, and veal are all charcoal-grilled much as they were at the gates of Troy by Agamemnon's soldiers. Beans and lentils, octopus and red mullet, oil and lemon, basil and oregano, figs and almonds, olives, and even the resinous taste of the wine, all form a gastronomic link between the worlds of ancient and modern Greece.

> Before ordering you can stroll into the kitchen and have a look at what's cooking.

Where to Eat

If possible, try to go where the Greeks go. In Rhodes and Kos, for instance, locals often keep away from crowded harbourside establishments. In a backstreet taverna, amongst people who will tolerate anything but bland food, you can enjoy the real zing of a garlicky yoghurt-and-cucumber *tsatsíki*. In the Old Town, stroll through the warren of the Jewish Quarter, and settle at a small taverna with rickety tables and chairs beneath a shady tree.

Look out for three types of snack bar. Yoghurt and cheese snacks are at the *galaktopolío* (dairy counter), while the *psistariá* (barbecue) serves different kinds of meat kebab, and usually fish. For a quick, satisfying, and economical snack, buy a *giros* at one of the stalls inside the New Market—spit-roasted lamb with *pítta* bread, onions, tomato, *tsatsíki,* and a variety of spices. Seats are in the form of wooden benches, where you can sit and make the food last, accompanied by a glass of beer.

A good selection of desserts can be found in a *zacharoplastío* (pastry shop)—there are lots of them under the arches of the New Market.

You'll come across the traditional Greek *kafenión* (café), particularly out in the villages, but this is more akin to a men's club than a public café, the typical *kafenión* being popular for political debate, backgammon, and extremely strong coffee. Although strangers are not refused admission, such places are considered, if not exactly off limits, at least a haven for Greeks among themselves.

When to Eat

If you do decide to "go Greek" and accept wholeheartedly the afternoon siesta institution, it will probably be necessary to modify your meal times accordingly. Greeks themselves put in a prolonged morning's work and have lunch around 2:00 P.M., followed by a siesta until 5:00 P.M., and then possibly some more work until 8:30 P.M. Usually, dinner is fairly late, not until 9:30 P.M. Restaurants will always serve you earlier, from midday and early evening, but you will miss the really authentic Greek scene if you choose to stick exclusively to "tourist hours."

The Menu

The tantalizing thing about the tasty Greek specialities we describe here is that only a fraction of them are available at any one time. Menus printed in English often list them all, but it is only those items with a price against them which are being served that day.

Rather than submit to this frustration, feel free to do what the locals do and take a trip into the kitchen to see what's being prepared. Cold appetizers are arrayed in display cases; cuts of meat and the fish of the day lie ready in glass-windowed refrigerators; and hot dishes are simmering on the stove in casseroles—the cook will lift the lid for you to peek in and sniff. The management is usually happy to point out choices here and therefore avoid misunderstandings later.

Remember that fish and meat are priced by weight; the size you pick in the kitchen is your responsibility when it becomes the bill. Agree on the weight before cooking, since it's hard to prove you haven't had 300 grams (10 ounces) of fish once it's gone.

Appetizers

It is the Greek custom to eat appetizers (*mezédes*) with an aperitif of *oúzo* and cold water, separately from the main meal. For convenience, they are usually served at resort tavernas as part of the dinner. But the essence of the *mezé* remains its leisurely enjoyment, something not to be gulped down before the main dish, but to be savoured in itself.

Besides the famous *tsatsíki*, there is an impressive range of *mezédes*, including: *taramá*, a creamy paste of cod's roe with breadcrumbs, egg yolk, olive oil, lemon juice, salt, and pepper; *dolmádes*, little parcels of vine leaves filled with rice and

Bread, wine, and a Greek salad are just the thing for an outdoor lunch at a shaded table.

sometimes minced mutton and pine kernels, braised in lemon and olive oil and served cold; *melitzanosaláta*, or aubergine (eggplant) salad puréed with onion and garlic; Greek salad (*saláta choriátiki*), a cool mixture of tomato, cucumber, *féta* cheese, and black olives; fried squid (*kalamaríkia tiganíta*) or marinated, cold octopus salad (*chtapódi*); cheese pies (*tirópitakia*), small triangles of pastry filled with goat and ewe cheese;

> **Vegetables are usually eaten cold (raw, or boiled, then cooled).**

mussels (*mithía*); and marinated mushrooms and white beans. Then, of course, there are always glistening black olives served by the dishful.

In many tavernas it is possible to order a selection of 10 or 15 *mezédes*, which sometimes are enough for a whole meal.

Fish

The Greek table's surest pleasure is its seafood, though this can be surprisingly expensive. The simplest method of cooking is the best: grilled sea bream (*fagrí*), swordfish (*xifías*), sole (*glóssa*), and red mullet (*barboúnia*) are a few of the most popular, but what is available depends on the day's catch. Fish is often accompanied by *skordalía*, a thick bread sauce powerfully flavoured with garlic. You may discover a host of other Greek fish with no generally accepted English names. If you like seafood stewed, try the octopus with white wine, potatoes, and tomatoes; or prawns (*garídes*) in white wine.

Meat

Tavernas usually serve garlic-marinated lamb kebabs with onions (*souvlákia*), and spicy, deep-fried meat balls (*keftédes*)—a real feast, especially if the lamb is minced with mint, onion, eggs, and bacon. If you order grilled steak (*brizóles*), it is likely to come well done unless you've

There's plenty of fish in the sea—no need to worry about not finding something to your taste.

specified otherwise, and is not usually tender enough to risk anything less than medium.

Two renowned Greek dishes are a good test of a restaurant's quality. *Moussaká* has as many variations as there are islands—and restaurants—but mainly consists of layers of chopped lamb, sliced aubergine, onions, and béchamel sauce. The more Italianate *pastitsío* uses lamb, mutton, or goat in alternating layers with macaroni, mixed variously with tomatoes, eggs, and cheese, and topped with a generous sprinkling of breadcrumbs. *Goúvetsi*, beef stewed in an earthenware pot with tiny lozenge-shaped noodles, is another popular casserole in the island's tavernas.

Cheeses

Cheese is generally made from ewe's or goat's milk. The best known soft cheese is *féta*, popping up in almost every Greek salad. *Kaserí*, a hard cheese, is best eaten fresh, but can also be used grated, like Parmesan, and in cooked dishes.

Desserts

The Greeks eat dessert at the neighborhood pastry shop. Tavernas rarely offer a large selection, though if you do ask for a dessert, the waiter might offer to nip out and buy you one.

The most popular all have honey in them, including: *pítta me melí,* honey cake; *kataïfi,* a sort of shredded wheat cake filled with honey and chopped almonds; *lou koú mades,* which is a doughnut-like honey fritter; and *baklavá,* that honey-drenched pastry with almonds and walnuts. Tavernas may be able to supply you with the perfect sour-sweet mixture of fresh, thick, creamy yoghurt and honey (*yaoúrti me melí*). This is sold in the dairy shops (*galaktopolió*) as well, which is where you'll find a Rhodian speciality, *rizógalo*—cold rice pudding flavoured with lemon and cinnamon. The best fruits are pomegranates, figs, grapes, peaches, apricots, and melons.

Coffee

Thick and syrupy, Greek coffee (*ellíniko*) is boiled to order in a long-handled pot, before being poured, grounds and all, into your cup. Ask for *éna varí glikó* if you want it heavy and sweet; *glikí vastró,* sweet but thinner; *éna métrio,* medium; or *éna skéto,* without sugar. Wait a few minutes before taking a sip, to allow the grounds to settle. The taste is strong, a bit like liquid liquorice. Many cafés and restaurants serve excellent espressos, and you can always ask for *nes,* instant coffee. Iced coffee, or *frappé,* is a popular hot-weather drink; it is also sold in plastic goblets in the supermarkets.

Wines and Spirits

As this is a duty-free island, you'll have no problem finding your favourite tipple, and at a very reasonable price. But there's no better place to sample *oúzo,* the national aperitif, than in a tree-shaded taverna by the sea. This clear, aniseed-flavoured spirit, reminiscent of French pastis, is usually mixed with cold water, which turns it a milky colour. Try it straight, skéto, or on the rocks, me págo, but drink it in moderation—it has a fair kick. You won't see Greeks drinking it without some kind of snack. The best of the Greek brandies (known locally as cognac—though there is no comparison with French brandy) are the dark, sweet Metaxá, the marginally drier Kambá, and the resinated Mastichá, which is drunk as an aperitif.

While away an afternoon in the Jewish Quarter.

Greek wine had a far better reputation in the ancient world than it does now. Fermented alcoholic drinks had preceded Greek civilization, but it was in fact the Greeks who turned the growing of vines into an agricultural practice, and who were the first to understand the importance of pruning plants and exploiting the dry, stony ground. The unique, resinous Retsína was a favourite of the ancient Greeks, and today pine resin is still added during fermentation to allow longer conservation in the climate. It only takes a few minutes to acquire the taste and learn how well it goes with both fish and meat.

Rhodes has been producing wine for many centuries. Most of its wines have the VQPRD label (denoting *vins de qualité produits aux régions déterminées,* or quality wines produced in specific regions). Free tastings are held regularly at the

CAIR cooperative on Kapodistrias Street in Rhodes Town, and the Emery winery in Émbonas.

The two most famous CAIR wines are the white *Ilíos* (dry) and red *Chevalier de Rhodes*, which some will have you believe the knights used to drink. Both *Ilíos* and *Chevalier* are simple table wines. Superior wines bear the Moulin label. CAIR also produce a good and sweet *Muscat de Rhodes*, and two sparkling wines, *Brut* and *Demi-sec*, both fermented by the *champenoise* method and sold all over Greece. They are gradually being introduced to the international market.

The other major wine producer is Emery, whose table wines are eminently drinkable—in particular the dry whites, produced from the indigenous Athiri grape. The dry *Villaré*, of which only 120,000 bottles are produced each year, a local legend. *Cava Emery* is a heady red, matured for many months in oak barrels and as well rated as many Burgundies. Emery also produce several sparkling wines, among them *cuvée close* and limited quantities of the *Grand Prix*, an excellent *méthode champenoise* wine.

To Help You Order

I'd like a/an/some…   **Tha íthela…**

beer	**mía bíra**	milk	**gála**
bread	**psomí**	mineral water	**metallikó neró**
coffee	**éna kafé**	pepper	**pipéri**
fish	**psári**	potatoes	**patátes**
fork	**éna piroúni**	rice	**rízi**
fruit	**froúta**	salad	**mía saláta**
glass	**éna potíri**	salt	**aláti**
ice-cream	**éna pagotó**	soup	**mía soúpa**
knife	**éna machéri**	sugar	**záchari**
lemon	**éna lemóni**	tea	**éna tsái**
meat	**kréas**	wine	**krasí**

INDEX

HANDY TRAVEL TIPS

An A–Z Summary of Practical Information

A

ACCOMMODATION (See also CAMPING on p. 104 and RECOMMENDED HOTELS on pp. 129–131)

Hotels (*xenodochío*) are classified in six official categories: Luxury at the top, then from A down to E. Rates are imposed by the government in all categories except Luxury, and they are posted behind each bedroom door. The Greek National Tourist Office can provide a brochure with a list of all hotels in Rhodes down to C category. However, such are the vagaries of Greek officialdom that the grades are not always a reliable guide to standards. A hotel which won its "A" category 30 years ago may now be run-down and surrounded by noisy discotheques, whereas a brand-new, quiet, welcoming hotel may merit only an "E" because it doesn't have a restaurant.

The most luxurious hotels are in Rhodes New Town or clustered along the west coast between Kritíka and Kremastí, from where they have views of the setting sun. Those along the east coast, which is developing more and more, have better beaches and excellent sports facilities. Generally, these hotels are well equipped, but are lacking in character. In Líndos, accommodation is mostly in the form of furnished apartments in restored traditional houses, which can be rented either through tour operators or on the spot if you come out of high season; there are two hotels at Vliha Bay, which is roughly 4 km (2½ miles) out of town.

The quietest and most atmospheric place to stay in Rhodes is the Old Town, which does not have luxury hotels but several friendly, family-run establishments in the lower grades, and reliable *pensions* where the only drawback is that you might have to share a bathroom.

If you go to Rhodes in high season (July–September), you'd be well advised to reserve a hotel room in advance. Either book in writing, or ask your travel agent to make the arrangements. If you do arrive without a room, either enquire at the Tourist Information Office at the airport or in Rimini Square, or follow one of the people who will accost you with offers of rooms when you disembark —they generally offer clean, inexpensive accommodation (*domátia*) in their own homes. You're under no obligation to accept if you don't like the room they show you.

I'd like a single/double room.	**Tha íthela éna monó/dipló domátio**
with bath/shower	**me bánio/dous**

AIRPORTS (*aerodrómio*)

Rhodes. All incoming flights land at the international airport at Paradísi, about 16 km (10 miles) from Rhodes Town. Formalities are kept to a minimum; sometimes there is only one official on duty. The taxi rank and bus stop are just outside the baggage claim area. Buses run to Rhodes Town centre. When returning to the airport, make sure to board a bus from West Side Bus Station heading for Paradísi. The airport has duty-free facilities, but not for passengers flying to other Greek destinations. If you want to book other flights, the Olympic Airways office is at 9, Ierou Lochou, Rhodes Town, tel. (0241) 24571/5 (reservations 0241 24555), open 8 am to 3:30 pm daily, except for Sunday.

Athens. Athens airport has two terminals: West, handling all Olympic Airways international and domestic flights (and thus flights to Rhodes), and East, for all other airlines. They are some distance apart, on opposite sides of the landing strips, and you will have to take a bus or taxi to get from one to the other. The blue-and-white express bus waits just outside the baggage claim area; before you put your luggage on board, buy a ticket from the kiosk —the bus has been known to leave with people's bags, leaving the owners behind and bewildered on the pavement. The taxi ride takes about 10 minutes, the bus up to 20 minutes, following a route among seemingly abandoned building sites. Be careful not to get on a bus bound for Piraeus or the centre of Athens. The West Terminal is somewhat rudimentary, so try to organize your trip to avoid long waits here.

C

CAMPING

Rhodes has two official campsites: one at Faliráki and a "deluxe" site on the coast at Lardos, near Líndos, with sports facilities and two swimming pools. You are not allowed to pitch a tent anywhere else.

CAR HIRE *(enikiázetai aftokiníton)* (See also DRIVING on page 107)

There are dozens of car-hire firms in town, along with agencies at the airport. It's wise to book a day in advance in high season, and it can be cheaper to reserve in advance from home. Cars can be delivered to the airport, the harbour, or your hotel. The deposit, which amounts to the estimated rental charge plus 20%, is waived for holders of recognized credit cards. Drivers should be at least 21, in some cases 23 or 24, depending on the firm and the type of car. An International Driving Permit, or a valid driver's licence from the country of residence, held for at least one year, is required. Third-party insurance is covered in the rates, but personal accident insurance and collision damage waiver are extra, and damage to tyres and the underside of the car is at your expense.

Rental agencies for scooters and motorbikes can be found around Platía Evréon Martíron in the Old Town, and many places in the New Town. Try out the vehicle to make sure it works properly before concluding an agreement. Don't be surprised if the scooters and motorbikes make a lot of noise; the Rhodians prefer debaffled exhaust pipes for reasons known only to themselves. In theory, no noise from two-wheeled vehicles is permitted during the siesta (2 pm–5 pm), after 11 pm, or in front of hotels, but no one seems to take heed of this. Under Greek law, it is an offence to drive without a crash helmet if the motorbike is over 50cc, but as the rental agencies do not have many available, everyone rides bare-headed. If you follow suit, be aware that you risk a fine.

CHILDREN'S RHODES

In addition to bountiful swimming opportunities in the summer, and Rhodes' beautiful parks, which are very suitable for keeping children occupied, some hotels have developed children's entertainment programmes. There are often games, sports, and events for children aged from 5–11 years.

CLIMATE

Unless you go to Rhodes in January or February, you can expect the weather to be sunny. July, August, and September are the hottest—and most crowded—months; December is the rainiest. The most pleasant time to go is perhaps the spring, when flowers bloom in profusion and the sun isn't too fierce.

		J	F	M	A	M	J	J	A	S	O	N	D
Air	°F	54	54	55	63	70	77	81	82	78	68	61	55
	°C	12	12	13	17	21	25	27	28	25	20	16	13
Water	°F	59	57	59	63	66	72	75	77	75	73	66	61
	°C	15	14	15	17	19	22	24	25	24	23	19	16
Rainy days		17	12	11	7	5	1	1	1	3	8	12	16

All figures are approximate monthly averages.

CLOTHING

Rhodes is very informal; people walk around the streets wearing the bare minimum. Ties are rarely required, and even for a prestigious performance at the National Theatre many men go in their shirt-sleeves (though the Greek women are glad of the occasion to don all their finery). However, remember that when visiting churches and monasteries, women are expected to cover themselves—no revealing necklines or shorts—or they will have to wait outside. Shorts for men, however, are considered acceptable. Dress for discos is usually quite smart, and in some hotels jackets are common in the evenings.

Dress and pack lightly; cotton is the best material for hot weather. There's often a breeze, so include a light jacket, and if you travel by boat, bring an anorak or warm cardigan, as the Aegean north wind, the *méltemi*, can be freezing, despite the sun.

Sturdy shoes are best for visiting archaeological sites, and flip-flops or thongs are good for pebble beaches and the sea bottom.

COMPLAINTS *(parápona)*

If you really feel you've been cheated or misled, take it up with the manager or owner of the establishment first. Although consumer protection is in its infancy in this country, Greeks are firm believers in fair play in commercial matters.

Still annoyed and unsatisfied? Go to see the tourist police (see Po- LICE on page 120), who should help you. Tourism is a major money-earner for the Greek government, and they want to keep you happy.

CONSULATES *(proxenío)*

If you run into trouble with the authorities or the police, get in touch with your consulate for advice. All the embassies are in Athens.

Britain: Amerikis Street, P.O. Box 47, Rhodes Town; tel. (0241) 27247.

USA: c/o Voice of America Radio; tel. 24731–3.

CRIME *(églima; klopí)*

Crime is practically nonexistent. Rhodes has no jail and has to send law-breakers (usually traffic offenders) to the island of Kos to be locked up. In most hotels you can rent a safe for your valuables, but there are few cases of items being taken from rooms.

CUSTOMS and ENTRY FORMALITIES

Visitors from EC countries need only an identity card to enter Greece, but it is recommended that a passport is also taken. Citizens of other countries must hold a valid passport. Certain prescription drugs, including tranquillizers and headache pain killers, may not be carried into the country without a prescription or official document. Surfboards and other equipment such as bicycles, water-skis, and so on, have to be registered in your passport upon arrival.

The following chart shows the quantities of certain items you may take into Greece and, upon your return home, into your own country. To be certain, ask for the customs form setting out allowances before your departure.

Currency restrictions. Non-residents may import up to 100,000 drachmas and export up to 10,000 drachmas, in denominations of up to 5,000. There's no limit on the foreign currency or travellers' cheques you may import, though amounts in excess of a value of $1,000 must be declared to the customs official upon arrival.

Into:	Cigarettes		Cigars		Tobacco	Spirits		Wine
Italy [1]	200	or	50	or	250g	1l	and	2l
Australia	200	or	250	or	250g	1l	or	1l
Canada	200	and	50	and	900g	1.1l	or	1.1l
Eire	200	or	50	or	250g	1l	and	2l
N Zealand	200	or	50	or	250g	1.1l	and	4.5l
S Africa	400	and	50	and	250g	1l	and	2l
UK	400	or	100	or	500g	1l	and	2l
USA	200	and	100	and	[2]	1l	or	1l
Within the EC [3]	800	and	200	and	1kg	10l	and	90l

1) For non-European residents or residents outside the EC or from duty-free shops within EC countries.

2) a reasonable quantity

3) Guidelines for non duty-free within the EC. For the import of larger amounts you must be able to prove that the goods are for your own personal use. For EC duty-free allowances see [1] above.

D

DRIVING

To bring your car into Greece you'll need the car registration papers, nationality plate or sticker, International Driving Permit (not required for British motorists), and comprehensive insurance coverage. When you enter Greece with your car (you'll be allowed six months) it will be registered in your passport. You won't be able to leave the country without your vehicle unless you go through a lengthy procedure to obtain a special paper withdrawing it from circulation. The standard red warning triangle is required in Greece for accidents and breakdowns. Seat belts are obligatory.

Motorways on mainland Greece are in good condition; tolls are calculated by distance. Roads are good in the north of Rhodes, but get progressively worse heading south: many are unsurfaced, and hazards to negotiate include pot-holes, donkeys, goats, stray dogs and cats, overhanging foliage, old ladies, and tourist coaches—so go carefully. Sound your horn when rounding blind corners; the Greeks hoot madly and merrily and expect the same from oncoming traffic.

Note that from March to October cars have unrestricted access to Rhodes Old Town only between 6 and 10 am. Traffic is forbidden between 10 am and 1:30 pm; from 1:30–5 pm only inhabitants of the Old Town may drive around. Everyone's cars are banned again from 5–9:30 pm, and from 9:30 pm–6 am only residents may use their cars. Some parking areas are reserved exclusively for locals.

Drive on the right, pass on the left. The speed limit on open roads is 90 km/h (50 mph), and in built-up areas 50 km/h (30 mph). Places of interest to tourists are signposted in English as well as Greek, and most road signs are standard pictographs used throughout Europe. In remote areas, however, it helps to have some knowledge of Greek script. You may encounter the following signs, written in Greek:

No through road	ΑΔΙΕΞΟΔΟΣ
Stop	ΑΛΤ
Bad road surface	ΑΝΩΜΑΛΙΑ ΟΔΟΣΤΡΩΜΑΤΟΣ
No waiting	ΑΠΑΓΟΡΕΥΕΤΑΙ Η ΑΝΑΜΟΝΗ
No entry	ΑΠΑΓΟΡΕΥΕΤΑΙ Η ΕΙΣΟΔΟΣ
No parking	ΑΠΑΓΟΡΕΥΕΤΑΙ Η ΣΤΑΘΜΕΥΣΙΣ
Reduce speed	ΕΛΑΤΤΩΣΑΤΕ ΤΑΧΥΤΗΤΑΝ
Dangerous incline	ΕΠΙΚΙΝΔΥΝΟΣ ΚΑΤΩΦΕΡΕΙΑ
Roadworks in progress	ΕΡΓΑ ΕΠΙ ΤΗΣ ΟΔΟΥ
Caution	ΚΙΝΔΥΝΟΣ

One-way traffic	ΜΟΝΟΔΡΟΜΟΣ
Diversion (detour)	ΠΑΡΑΚΑΜΠΤΗΡΙΟΣ
Cyclists	ΠΟΔΗΛΑΤΑΙ
Keep right	ΠΟΡΕΙΑ ΥΠΟΧΡΕΩΤΙΚΗ ΔΕΞΙΑ
Bus stop	ΣΤΑΣΙΣ ΛΕΩΦΡΕΙΟΥ

In the event of an accident or breakdown, you could contact the car-rental agency, or the following numbers may be useful:

Motorist's Road Assistance (ELPA), tel. 104

Emergency service, tel. 100

Traffic Police, tel. (0241) 22344/23329

Tourist Police, tel. (0241) 27423

Fuel and oil. Service stations are plentiful on the island, but fill up before heading for the more remote areas in the south. Opening hours are 7 am–7 pm, and one station in a radius of 14 km (8½ miles) is open until midnight on a rotation basis—its name is displayed at each service station, or telephone the tourist police (0241) 27423. You can get normal petrol (gasoline) (84–86 octane), super (92–95 octane), lead-free, and diesel.

Fluid measures

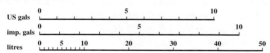

Distance

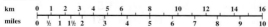

Distances from Rhodes Town. Archángelos 32 km (20 miles); Émbonas 55 km (34 miles); Kámiros 34 km (21 miles); Kataviá (along east coast) 87 km (54 miles); Líndos 55 km (34 miles); Monólithos 66 km (41 miles); Petaloúdes 24 km (15 miles).

Rhodes

Are we on the right road for…?	**Ímaste sto sostó drómo giá…?**
Full tank, please.	**Na to gemísete me venzíni.**
normal/super/lead-free	**aplí/soúper/amólivdos**
Check the oil/tyres/battery.	**Na elénxete ta ládia/ta lásticha/ti bataría.**
My car has broken down.	**Épatha mía vlávi.**
There's been an accident.	**Égine éna distíchima.**

E

ELECTRIC CURRENT

You'll find only 220-volt, 50-cycle AC current. Sockets are two- or three-pin. If you want to use your own appliances, it will probably be worth your while buying an international adapter.

an adapter	**énas metaschimatistís**
a battery	**mía bataría**

EMERGENCIES

Except in very remote areas, you'll usually find someone who speaks English and will be able to help you. In case of emergency, here are a few essential telephone numbers:

Police and Emergency Services	100
First Aid	22222
Tourist Police	23329/27423
Fire Brigade	199
Port Police	27695/28888

Some useful expressions:

Careful!	**Prosochí!**	Help!	**Voíthia!**
Fire!	**Fotiá!**	Stop!	**Stamatíste!**

G

GETTING to RHODES

By air: A large number of tour operators offer holidays in Rhodes in both their winter and summer programmes. Prices vary enormously according to the season, type of flight (scheduled or charter airline), and the standard of hotel. Pick up as many brochures as you can to compare prices, and look carefully at the location of hotels available; your choice will depend on whether you want to be in town or on a beach, in a hotel or furnished apartment, somewhere quiet or busy.

Charter flights fly directly to Rhodes from many provincial airports in Britain; on scheduled flights you will have to change planes in Athens (see AIRPORTS on page 103). There are several Olympic Airways flights between Athens and Rhodes every day in summer, but fewer in winter; the trip takes about 45 minutes. Special excursion fares are available. If you can plan and pay far enough in advance, APEX (advance purchase excursion) or ABC (advance booking charter) fares can mean even greater savings.

Rhodes also has direct air links with Iráklion, Kárpathos, Kásos, Kastellórizo, Kos, Mykonós, Mytilini (Lesbos), Paros, Santoríni, Sitía, and Thessaloniki (Salonica). (Mykonós and Santoríni only from April to October.)

By sea: International sea routes connect Rhodes with Turkey, Cyprus, Israel, and Egypt. Vessels operating on these routes are generally large passenger ships, many of which carry cars. Your travel agent or the Mandráki tourist office will have the latest information on sailing times. In addition, car ferries and passenger boats operate between Rhodes and Piraeus, with at least one per day during the summer. Some ferries to Rhodes make several stops along the way, taking 19 hours to get there, but one, the *Rodos*, operates direct and completes the Piraeus–Rhodes run in about 14 hours. Prices on these island boats are reasonable, but the older boats can be uncomfortable.

Rhodes

There are daily sailings, by boat or hydrofoil, from Rhodes to and from Kos, Kálymnos, Léros, Pátmos and Symi. Car ferries also run to Turkey (Marmaris), Cyprus and Israel (Haifa).

By Road: One way of getting to Rhodes is by road and then ferry— whether you choose to drive to one of the Italian ports or directly to Piraeus via Athens—but this is certainly neither the fastest, nor the most convenient way of reaching the island. Allow at least four to five days; and only with several people sharing a car might it work out cheaper than a charter flight. The most direct route to Athens is via Frankfurt–Munich–Graz–Belgrade–Skopje—approximately 3,200 km (2,000 miles) from the Channel ports. The route via Italy and then by the Ancona–Patras ferry is easier.

Cross-Channel ferry and hovercraft space is at a premium in summer, so make sure you have a reservation. Hovercraft service between Dover and Calais takes about 35 minutes. Car-ferry routes link Dover–Calais, Newhaven–Dieppe, Portsmouth–Le Havre, Weymouth–Cherbourg, Plymouth–Roscoff and Rosslaire–Le Havre or Cherbourg.

Some coach operators offer excursions from London and Continental Europe to Athens in summer.

By rail: Given the outstanding problems in Yugoslavia it is probably wiser to travel to Greece through Italy to Brindisi and take the ferry to Patras from there.

Eurailpasses are special rover tickets covering most of Western Europe (including Greece), for non-European residents only, to be purchased before leaving home. The *Inter-Rail-Card* allows either 15 days or one month of unlimited 2nd-class rail travel on all participating European railways in 19 countries (including Greece). It is currently available for adults over 26. The under-26 version can now be bought for restricted zones at a lower price, or you can still choose the all-zone "pan-European" option. The *Eurodomino Freedom Pass* allows unlimited travel on 3, 5, or 10 days in a month, in the country or countries of your choice.

L

LANGUAGE

The table below lists the Greek letters in their capital and lower case forms, followed by the letters they correspond to in English. In cases where pronunciation varies, we have given examples.

Unfortunately, there's no consistency in the way the Greeks transcribe their language. The word *ágios* (saint), for example, is often spelt *ághios* or *áyios* (with the letter "g" pronounced as **y** in **y**et). There is similar confusion between "d" and "t," "i" and "y," "b" and "v," "u," and "ou." Stress is an important feature of Greek. It is usually indicated by an acute accent (´) over the vowel of the syllable to be stressed, though the Greeks themselves don't bother with this over capital letters or when transcribing addresses. Throughout this guide we have shown stresses on words and phrases.

A	α	a	as in b**a**t
B	β	v	
Γ	γ	g	as in **g**o
Δ	δ	d	like **th** in **th**is
E	ε	e	as in g**e**t
Z	ζ	z	as in ja**zz**
H	η	i	like **ee** in m**ee**t
Θ	θ	th	as in **th**in
I	ι	i	like **ee** in m**ee**t
K	κ	k	
Λ	λ	l	
M	μ	m	
N	ν	n	
Ξ	ξ	x	like **ks** in than**ks**
O	o	o	as in h**o**t
Π	π	p	
P	ρ	r	
Σ	σ,ς	s	as in ki**ss**

T	τ	t	
Y	υ	i	like **ee** in m**ee**t
Φ	φ	f	
X	χ	ch	as in Scottish lo**ch**
Ψ	ψ	ps	as in ti**ps**y
Ω	ω	o	as in b**o**ne
OY	ου	ou	as in s**ou**p

The Berlitz phrasebook GREEK FOR TRAVELLERS covers most situations you are likely to encounter on your travels in Greece. We have included a number of useful expressions in this book—see page 127 and the inside front cover.

LAUNDRY and DRY-CLEANING *(plintírio; katharistírio)*

Some hotels may take care of your laundry. If not, there is a coin-operated laundrette in the New Town, at 28 Octovriou. There are also a couple of dry-cleaners in the area.

When will it be ready?	**Póte tha íne étimo?**
I must have this for tomorrow morning.	**Prépi na íne étimo ávrio to proí.**

LOST PROPERTY *(grafío apolesthéndon andikiménon)*

If you've lost or mislaid something, don't worry too much—you have a good chance of getting it back. Return to where you think you lost it, or call the Lost and Found Office, tel. (0241) 23294.

I've lost my wallet/handbag/ passport.	**Échasa to portofóli mou/ti tsánda mou/to diavatirió mou.**

MAPS *(chártis)*

There are several maps of the island on sale in newspaper kiosks. They are not dated, and some of them are quite antiquated; try to find one marked "New Edition," though even this is not a guarantee of reliability, as old mistakes are recopied year after year.

MEDIA

Newspapers and magazines *(efimerída; periodikó)* Most foreign dailies—including the principal British newspapers and the Paris-based *International Herald Tribune*—arrive on Rhodes one day after publication. For the biggest selection, go to the news-stand in the main entrance to the New Market on Mandráki Harbour, or the Presbyran newsagents on Griva Street, where you'll also find a few English paperbacks. Your Sunday newspaper may come minus its colour supplement. For faster news in English, pick up the *Athens News*. The free, English-language *Rodos News*, published monthly, is available at the tourist office and most hotel reception desks.

Radio and TV *(rádio; tileórasi).* Rhodes has its own English-language radio station, Rhodes 95.9 International, broadcasting every afternoon, seven days a week. It provides local, world, and sports news, holiday information, cultural events, and popular music. Greek National Radio broadcasts news in English from Monday to Friday around 7:40 am in the summer season. You can also tune in to TRT (Turkish Radio) which gives the news in English, French, and German, every other hour on the hour. This is the best programme for classical music. The Voice of America operates a relay transmitter on Rhodes, just outside the village of Koskinoú. While most broadcasting is in Arabic and Turkish, a world-news summary in English is given from 6–7 pm.

MEDICAL CARE

The sun is much stronger than you think—do your eyes a favour and wear good sunglasses. Sunbathe only for short periods for the first few days—no more than an hour per day—and stay out of the sun between 11 am and 2 pm. Even people who believe they have sun-resistant skin should coat themselves liberally with a high-factor, oil-based lotion. Take particular care with young children; and drink plenty of water. If you do get burnt, try the local remedy: yoghurt. Smear it on, leave it as long as you like, then shower it off.

Rhodes

You can buy lotions or essential oils to repel mosquitoes, but they have to be reapplied every two to three hours to remain effective. To keep mosquitoes out of your room, buy an electrical repellent that plugs into a wall socket.

Make sure your health-insurance policy covers any illness or accident while on holiday. There are many competent English-speaking doctors, specialists, and dentists on Rhodes, most of them centred in the New Town around the Olympic Airways office. You'll have to pay a small consultation fee; keep the receipts for your insurance claims. Pharmacies (*farmakíon*) have a wide range of products, and there's always one open all night and on Sunday. Pharmacists are allowed to sell antibiotics without a prescription, and they are a good source of advice regarding minor medical problems. The hospital (*nosokomío*) is open 24 hours a day for emergencies, tel. (0241) 22222.

| a doctor/a dentist | **énas giatrós/énas odontogiatrós** |
| an ambulance | **éna asthenofóro** |

MONEY MATTERS

The monetary unit of Greece is the drachma (*drachmí*, abbreviated "drs"). There are coins of 1, 2, 5, 10, 20, 50, and 100 drachmas, and notes in denominations of 50, 100, 500, 1,000, and 5,000 drachmas.

Banks and currency exchange offices (*trápeza; sinállagma*). The leading Greek banks have branch offices in both New and Old towns, and there is a Barclays Bank at Polytechniou 3.

Banking hours are Monday to Thursday 8 am–2 pm, Friday 8 am–1:30 pm. The National Bank of Greece opens for currency exchange on Monday to Thursday afternoons 6–8, Friday 3–8:30 pm, Saturday, Sunday, and holidays 9 am–noon. You can also change money in hotels and at travel agencies; the rates are displayed on the desk. Travellers' cheques and Eurocheques will get a better rate than cash. Always take your passport with you when you go to exchange money.

Credit cards (*pistotikí kárta*). Recognized cards are honoured in most shops and by all banks, car-hire firms, and leading hotels in Rhodes; but take Greek currency for dining out in local tavernas.

Do you accept travellers' cheques? **Pérnete "traveller's cheques"?**

Can I pay with this credit card? **Boró na pliróso me aftí ti pistotikí kárta?**

PLANNING YOUR BUDGET

To give you an idea of what to expect, here are some average prices in Greek drachmas. However, all prices should be regarded only as *approximate*, as they tend to rise ever higher in the tourist season.

Airport transfer. Public bus to Rhodes Town 500 drs, taxi 1,600–2,000 drs. Athens, taxi between East and West terminals 1,000 drs, express bus 160 drs.

Bicycle and motorscooter hire. Bicycles 800–1,500 drs per day, motorscooters 5,000–10,000 drs per day.

Buses. Rhodes Town to Líndos 800 drs, to Kallithéa 500 drs, to Faliráki 500 drs, to Monólithos 1,050 drs.

Car hire (July–October). *Fiat Panda* (limited 100 km/60 miles mileage) 16,000 drs per day (including insurance but plus 13% VAT), 50 drs per km; (unlimited mileage) 20,000 drs (including insurance and VAT). *Suzuki jeep* (limited 100 km/60 miles mileage) 23,000 drs per day (including insurance but plus VAT), 60 drs per km; (unlimited mileage) 26,000 drs per day (including insurance and VAT).

Cigarettes. Greek brands 250–380 drs per packet of 20, foreign brands 600 drs.

Entertainment. *Bouzoúki* evening: including drink 3,000–4,000 drs, including food 6,000–8,000 drs; discotheque (admission and first drink) 2,500–3,000 drs.

Excursions. Day trip to Symi 3,000 drs, to Kos (hydrofoil) 8,500 drs (round trip).

Hairdressers. Woman's haircut starting at 5,000 drs, shampoo and set starting at 3,500 drs. Man's haircut starting at 4,000 drs.

Rhodes

Hotels (double room with bath per night in high season, and including breakfast and all taxes). De luxe 25,000–37,000 drs, Class A 20,000–30,000 drs, Class B 13,000–22,000 drs, Class C 9,000–18,000 drs, Class D 4,500–9,000 drs.

Meals and drinks. Continental breakfast 500–800 drs, lunch or dinner in fairly good establishment 1,200–4,400 drs, beer 600–800 drs, coffee 400–700 drs, soft drink 300–1,500 drs, Greek 3-star brandy (in bar) 200–1,200 drs.

Petrol (gasoline). Super 200 drs per litre, regular 184 drs per litre, unleaded 198 drs per litre.

Photo developing. To develop a roll of 36 colour exposures, approximately 3,000 drs depending on the size of print. You'll probably get a free film as well.

Shopping. Ready-made salads (100g): *taramasaláta* 280 drs, tuna 450 drs, aubergine 413 drs; 500g *féta* cheese 550–650 drs; 100g ham 250 drs; 100g salami 210 drs; 6 eggs 190 drs; packet cornflakes 400–650 drs; 750g honey 670 drs; 500g Greek marmalade 195 drs; 560g tin black olives 550 drs; 1kg oranges 200–300 drs; melon 300–350 drs per kg; 500g strawberries 300 drs; 1.5-litre bottle mineral water 90–150 drs; 1 litre orange juice 390 drs; 260g Nescafé 950 drs.

Sports. Dinghy 5,000 drs per hour. Water-skiing 3,000 drs for 10 minutes. Tennis 2,500–3,000 drs per couple per hour (including racket and balls).

Video camera tax (at archaeological sites). The charge varies according to the location.

OPENING HOURS

As opening hours of many establishments are lengthened during the tourist season, we advise that you check first.

Banks: Monday to Thursday 8 am–2 pm, Friday 8 am–1:30 pm.

Churches and museums: As opening times vary enormously among churches and museums, it is recommended that you check with each individual establishment before setting out. In peak season (June to September), opening hours are often lengthened in order to accommodate tourists.

Currency exchange: normal banking hours. The National Bank of Greece also exchanges currency Monday to Friday 5–8:30 pm, Saturday, Sunday and holidays 9 am –noon.

Hairdressers: Monday to Friday 9 am –9 pm; Saturday 9 am–8 pm; Sunday and holidays 9 am–noon.

OTE (telephone office): 7:30 am–11 pm.

Pharmacies: Weekdays 8 am–2 pm, 6–8 pm; Saturday 8 am–2 pm. Outside these hours, see the notice posted in the window of any pharmacy indicating the nearest one on duty.

Post Office: Monday to Friday 7:30 am–8 pm.

Shops: Monday and Wednesday 9 am–5 pm; Tuesday, Thursday, and Friday 10 am–7 pm; Saturday 8 am–1 pm; closed Sunday.

Tourist Office: 8 am–7:30 pm; closed Sunday.

Tourist shops: 9 am–10 pm; Sunday 10 am–2 pm.

P

PHOTOGRAPHY and VIDEO

There are plenty of photo shops where you can have films developed quickly—some even claim to need only 23 minutes. If you decide to wait until you get home, store your films somewhere cool until then. Most brands of colour and black-and-white film are available.

Video cameras can be used on the archaeological sites, but you'll have to pay an exorbitant fee for the privilege. Tripods are also subject to entry fees as they are considered the mark of a professional.

For security reasons, it is illegal to use a telephoto lens aboard an aircraft flying over Greece, and on the runway at Rhodes Airport.

Rhodes

POLICE (*astinomía*)

Regular police (*chorofílakes*) wear green uniforms. They are particularly severe on people caught speeding and can impose fines on the spot. The Tourist Police (*touristikí astinomía*) are a special branch, with the authority to inspect prices in hotels. They have a dark grey uniform, with flags sewn on indicating the foreign languages they speak. These are the people to turn to if you have a problem or complaint. For the traffic police and emergency services, tel. **100**; for the tourist police (0241) 27423; for the port police (0241) 27695 or (0241) 28888.

Where's the nearest police station?	**Pou íne to kodinótero astinomikió tmíma?**

POST OFFICES

The main post and telegraph office (*tachidrómio*), an imposing building facing Mandráki Harbour, is open Monday to Friday 7:30 am–8 pm (closed Saturday). There are also three sub-post offices, on Orféos in the Old Town, at Faliráki, and opposite the Rhodes Palace Hotel, open Monday to Friday 8 am–2 pm from May to October. You can purchase stamps wherever you buy postcards. If you have mail addressed to you *poste restante* (general delivery), it will arrive at the main post office; take your passport for identification.

There are no public fax facilities, but you could ask at your hotel or at a travel agency to use theirs.

A stamp for this letter/postcard, please.	**Ena grammatosimo giafto to gramma/kart postal, parakalo.**
I want to send a telegram to …	**Thélo na stílo éna tilegráfima sto …**
Have you received any mail for …?	**Échete grámmata giá …?**

PUBLIC HOLIDAYS (*argíes*)

Banks, offices, and shops close on the following national holidays:

January 1	*Protochroniá*	New Year's Day

January 6	*ton Theofaníon*	Epiphany
March 25	*Ikosti Pémti Martíou (tou Evangelismoú)*	Greek Independence Day
May 1	*Protomagiá*	May Day
August 15	*Dekapendávgoustos (tis Panagías)*	Assumption Day
October 28	*Ikosti Ogdóï Oktovríou*	Óchi ("No") Day, commemorating Greek defiance of Italian ultima- tum and invasion of 1940
December 25	*Christoúgenna*	Christmas Day
December 26	*défteri iméra ton Christougénnon*	St. Stephen's Day

Movable dates:

Katharí Deftéra	1st day of Lent: Clean Monday
Megáli Paraskeví	Good Friday
Deftéra tou Páscha	Easter Monday
Análipsis	Ascension day
tou Agíou Pnévmatos	Whit Monday ("Holy Spirit")

The dates on which movable holy days are celebrated follow the Orthodox calendar, and often differs from those elsewhere.

PUBLIC TRANSPORT

Boats and ferries. Departures from Rhodes are best discovered on the spot, either at the National or Municipal Tourist Offices, in one of the agencies that proliferate all over town, or by phoning the port police, tel. (0241) 28888 or (0241) 27695.

Hydrofoils and day-trip boats from Mandráki Harbour run regularly; tickets can be bought on the harbour, in one of the agencies, and at some hotel reception desks. Inter-island car ferries leave from Emborió, the Commercial harbour. They are fairly reliable, but tend to depend on weather conditions—some parts of the Aegean can get very choppy. Chaos reigns at the Emborió ticket office, which is in reality a table set up whenever needed in the self-service restaurant. No official timetable is posted there, none of the officials wandering around with guns and walkie-talkies seem to know what time any boat is going to arrive, and there's nothing to tell you where to wait. People just sit around, propped up by their backpacks, hoping.

Buses (*leoforío*). The island has reliable, inexpensive bus services. The main station in Rhodes Town stretches along the side of the road from the Tourist Information Office opposite the New Market back along Papágou. It's divided into East Side, at the front, and West Side, behind. A left-luggage office is in a building on the opposite side of the road. Timetables (copies available) are posted on the window of the Tourist Information Office. Every bus stop also has a very detailed timetable, extremely well organized in that it indicates the time the bus leaves the Rimini Square terminus, the time it arrives at that particular stop, and the return times from the destination point. The timetables are drawn up to suit islanders rather than tourists, reaching town early in the morning and home again in the afternoon.

If you get on the bus at a terminus, the conductor will come round issuing tickets. Otherwise, board at the rear and pay the conductor, who will be sitting behind a little cash desk. Keep your ticket until the end of your trip, as an inspector might get on to check.

R

RELIGION (*litourgía*)

The national church of Greece is Greek Orthodox. There's no Anglican or other Protestant congregation on Rhodes, but consult the notice board outside St. Mary's Catholic Church, Kathopouli 45, Rhodes Town, since visiting clergymen sometimes conduct Protestant services there. At St. Mary's, mass is said on weekdays at 7 pm, and on Sundays at 8 am, 11am, and 7 pm. At St. Francis' Church, Dimokratías 28, mass is said during the week at 8:30 pm, on Saturday at 6 pm, and on Sunday at 10 am. The mass is said in Latin or Greek. There is a synagogue on Dosiádou in Rhodes Town (see page 44).

T

TAXIS *(taxí)*

There are two kinds of taxi drivers on Rhodes: nasty ones who won't drive you and your luggage to your hotel in the back streets of the Old Town, and nice ones who will. If happen on the first kind, it is best to ask him to put you down at the gate in the ramparts nearest to your hotel, and walk the rest of the way. The majority of drivers, however, are helpful and honest, and prices are inexpensive.

The *agoréon* is a kind of taxi that functions outside the city limits. There is no meter, but rates are fixed for specific distances or zones, working out slightly higher than meter prices. It's quite common for people to share a taxi; hiring one for the day or several hours is subject to negotiation—agree on the price before you set off.

The main rank in Rhodes Town is in front of the bus station, opposite the New Market. To get a taxi, tel. (0241) 27666, or telephone Radio-Taxis, tel. (0241) 64712 or (0241) 64734. Tip about 10%, or round up the fare.

What's the fare to…?	**Piá íne í timí giá…?**
Could you give me a receipt?	**Miá apóthiksi parákalo?**

TELEPHONES *(tiléfono)*

The Greek telephone system could hardly be called efficient. You often have to dial several times before you can get through to your number, and every evening the lines are overloaded. There is a seven-year waiting list for private telephones on Rhodes, so most people make their calls from newspaper kiosks (*períptero*) or from the telephone centre of the Greek Telecommunications Organization (OTE), on the corner of Amerikis and 25 Martiou in the New Town, a block inland from the post office. There are other OTE offices very close to the sub-post offices (see POST OFFICES on page 120).

All public phone booths are now cardphones. Long-distance calls can be made here. You will need to buy a card (100 units available from kiosks; 500 and 1,000 units from the OTE). Many hotels have direct-dialling phones, but they often mark up the rates for international calls.

Rhodes

Useful numbers (see also EMERGENCIES on page 110):

Directory Information   131

International Telephone Information   161

Some country codes:

Australia	0061	South Africa	0027
Canada	001	United Kingdom	0044
Eire	00353	United States	001
New Zealand	0064		

TIME DIFFERENCES

Since Greece switches to Summer Time around the same date as Great Britain, there's a two-hour difference between the countries all year round. Here's the normal time difference in summer:

Los Angeles	Chicago	New York	London	**Rhodes**
2 am	4 am	5 am	10 am	**noon**

TIPPING

By law, service charges are included in the bill at hotels, restaurants, and tavernas, but if the service has been good, there's nothing to stop you leaving a little more. Even if your room or meals are included as part of a package tour, you'll still want to remember the maid and the waiter. The waiter will probably have a *mikró* (assistant) who should be given something as well.

Hotel porter, per bag	30–50 drs
Maid, per day	100 drs
Waiter	5% (optional)
Lavatory attendant	20 drs
Taxi driver	10% (optional)
Tour guide	100–200 drs (optional)
Hairdresser/Barber	10%

TOILETS

There are plenty of public conveniences on the island—in varying degrees of pungency and indicated by big hand-painted signs proclaiming "WC." Those on Rimini Square and in the centre of the New Market in Rhodes Town are scrupulously clean, guarded by old ladies sitting beneath a sign, "Not Pay," who dole out pieces of toilet paper. Give them a few coins if you want to avoid a fierce glare when you come out. On Rhodes, as on most Greek islands, the plumbing system easily gets choked up. That's why on every toilet you'll see a hand-written notice stating "Please do not put anything in the toilet" or "Please put everything in the bin provided." These warnings shouldn't be taken *too* literally—the toilets do work, but cannot cope with paper. Everyone is so used to this system that even when there isn't a bin, "everything" is heaped up on the floor in a corner.

You can, of course, use the toilets in cafés and restaurants providing you're a customer, and in an emergency, if you're brazen enough, try the nearest hotel.

TOURIST INFORMATION OFFICES

The City of Rhodes Tourist Information Office on Rimini Square (tel. (0241) 35945) is staffed with efficient multilingual personnel. They can provide information on local excursions, buses and ferries, and museum opening hours. The office is open six days a week during the summer, from 8 am to 7 pm weekdays, Saturday 8 am–6 pm. They always have copies of the *Rodos News*, *Rodos Kurier*, *Rodoksen Sanomat,* and *Rodos Bladet*, the island's free, foreign-language newspapers.

The central headquarters of the National Tourist Organization of Greece (GNTO) (*Ellinikós Organismós Tourismoú*, abbreviated EOT) is in Athens at Amerikis 2; tel. 3223–1119. In Rhodes Town, the GNTO is situated on the corner of Makaríou and Papágou streets, open Monday to Friday from 7:30 am to 3 pm; tel. (0241) 23255/(0241) 23655.

Outside the country, the offices below will supply you with a wide range of colourful and informative brochures and maps in

Rhodes

English. They will also let you consult the master directory of hotels in Greece, listing all facilities and prices.

Britain: GNTO, 4 Conduit Street, London WIR ODJ; tel. (0171) 734-5997.

USA: GNTO, 645 Fifth Avenue, 5th Floor, New York, NY 10022; tel. (212) 421-5777; 611 W 6th Street, Los Angeles, CA 90017; tel. (213) 626-6696; 168 N Michigan Avenue, Suite 600, Chicago, IL 60601; tel. (312) 782-1084.

Canada: GNTO, 1300 Bay Street, Toronto, Ont. M5R 3K8 tel. (416) 968-2220; 1233 rue de la Montagne, Suite 101, Montreal, Que. H3G 1Z2; tel. (514) 871-1535.

TRAVELLERS with DISABILITIES

Unfortunately, facilities for the disabled on Rhodes are far from ample. At the airport there is a bus with a special platform which transfers disabled people from the ground into the aeroplane, but in general throughout the island public services and streets are not designed with disabled people in mind. For any further information, contact the tourist information office (see page 125).

W

WATER *(neró)*

Not only is tap water safe to drink, but village connoisseurs debate over the special qualities and the taste of particular springs. Greeks usually serve water as a chaser for alcoholic drinks and coffee. Bottled mineral water—local brands as well as well-known French names—is also available in bars, restaurants, supermarkets, and "Tourist Shops."

a bottle of mineral water	**éna boukáli metallikó neró**
fizzy (carbonated)	**me anthrakikó**
still	**chorís anthrakikó**
Is this drinking water?	**Íne pósimo aftó to neró?**

WEIGHTS AND MEASURES

(For fluid and distance measures, see DRIVING on page 107.)

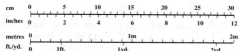

Length

cm	0	5	10	15	20	25	30
inches	0	2	4	6	8	10	12
metres	0		1m				2m
ft./yd.	0	1ft.	1yd.			2yd.	

Weight

| grams | 0 | 100 | 200 | 300 | 400 | 500 | 600 | 700 | 800 | 900 | 1kg |
| ounces | 0 | 4 | 8 | 12 | 1lb | 20 | 24 | 28 | 2lb | | |

Temperature

| °C | -30 -25 -20 -15 -10 -5 0 5 10 15 20 25 30 35 40 45 |
| °F | -20 -10 0 10 20 30 40 50 60 70 80 90 100 110 |

SOME USEFUL EXPRESSIONS

For further useful expressions, please see the inside front cover of this guide.

Good afternoon	**kalispéra**
Good night	**kaliníchta**
Goodbye	**yássas/yássou/ádio**
How are you?	**Ti kánete?**
Fine, thanks.	**Kalá, efcháristo.**
OK	**endáksi**
where/when/how	**pou/póte/pos**
how long/how far	**póso keró/póso makriá**
yesterday/today/tomorrow	**chthes/símera/ávrio**
day/week/month/year	**iméra/evdomáda/minás chrónos**
left/right	**aristerá/dexiá**
up/down	**epáno/káto**
good/bad	**kalós/kakós**
big/small	**megálos/mikrós**
cheap/expensive	**fthinós/akrivós**

Rhodes

hot/cold	**zestós/kríos**
old/new	**paliós/néos**
open/closed	**aniktós/klistós**
Please write it down.	**Parakaló grápste to.**
Call a doctor—quickly!	**Kaléste éna yiatró—grígora!**
What do you want?	**Ti thélete?**
Just a minute.	**Éna leptó.**

Days of the Week

Sunday	**Kiriakí**	Thursday	**Pémbti**
Monday	**Deftéra**	Friday	**Paraskeví**
Tuesday	**Tríti**	Saturday	**Sávvato**
Wednesday	**Tetárti**		

Months

January	**Ianouários**	July	**Ioúlios**
February	**Fevrouários**	August	**Ávgoustos**
March	**Mártios**	September	**Septémvrios**
April	**Aprílios**	October	**Októvrios**
May	**Máïos**	November	**Noémvrios**
June	**Ioúnios**	December	**Dekémvrios**

Numbers

1	**éna**	13	**dekatría**	50	**penínda**
2	**dío**	14	**dekatéssera**	60	**exínda**
3	**tría**	15	**dekapénde**	70	**evdomínda**
4	**téssera**	16	**dekaéxi**	80	**ogdónda**
5	**pénde**	17	**dekaeptá**	90	**enenínda**
6	**éxi**	18	**dekaoktó**	100	**ekató**
7	**eftá**	19	**dekaenniá**	101	**ekatón éna**
8	**októ**	20	**íkosi**	102	**ekatón dío**
9	**enniá**	21	**íkosi éna**	500	**pendakósia**
10	**déka**	30	**triánda**	1,000	**chília**
11	**éndeka**	31	**triánda éna**	5,000	**pénde chiliades**
12	**dódeka**	40	**saránda**	10,000	**déka chiliades**

Recommended Hotels

At last inspection, the following hotels all met with reasonable standards of cleanliness and comfort. They are listed alphabetically, according to price and geographical location. Most of the accommodation in Líndos consists of furnished apartments or villas, generally booked solid through tour operators during high season. If you would like to stay there, try your luck with a reliable travel agent in Líndos.

Greek hotels are classified by the government in six categories, from Luxury to E class (see page 102). Room prices are government controlled and increase slightly during high season. As a basic guide, we have used the following symbols for a double room with bath or shower:

✪	below 6,000 drs.
✪✪	6,000–10,000 drs.
✪✪✪	above 10,000 drs.

Rhodes, Old Town

S. Nikolis Hotel ✪✪✪ *Ippodámou 61, 85100 Rhodes; Tel. (0241) 34561; Fax (0241) 32034.* Lovely hotel in a quiet location, covered in creepers. Some rooms with balcony overlooking garden. Roof-top terrace, oúzeria.

Pension Massari ✪ *Irodótou 42, 85100 Rhodes; Tel. (0241) 22469.* Very close to the walls, at the back of the Old Town. Walk towards the end of Ippodámou or Omírou, or enter the walls through St. Athanasius' Gate, and look for the sign on the wall.

Pension Steve ✪ *Omírou 60, 85100 Rhodes; Tel. (0241) 24357.* Quiet, inexpensive, with charming garden, on one of the Old Town's most atmospheric streets.

Sydney Hotel ✪ *Apellou 41, 85100 Rhodes; Tel. (0241) 25965.* Cheap pension in the Old Town, just off Sokrátous and surrounded by low-priced bars and tavernas.

Rhodes, New Town

Adonis Pension ✪✪ *7 Vassleos Konstandinou, 85100 Rhodes; Tel. (0241) 27791.* Attractive town house located opposite the old Hotel della Rosa. Easy access to aquarium and Elli beach, and a pretty garden patio.

Constantin Hotel ✪✪✪ *Amerikis 65, 85100 Rhodes; Tel. (0241) 22971; Fax (0241) 30379.* Situated close to the beach and all amenities, offering 139 rooms, all with balcony. Convivial bar and restaurant. Category B.

Grand Hotel Rhodes ✪✪✪✪ *Akti Miaouli 1, 85100 Rhodes; Tel. (0241) 26284; Fax (0241) 35589.* Regarded by many as the "grandest" hotel in Rhodes Town, and well positioned on the west shore, affording fabulous views of the setting sun. All amenities.

Ibiscus Hotel ✪✪✪ *Nissirou 17, 85100 Rhodes; Tel. (0241) 24421; Fax (0241) 27283.* Excellent, A-category hotel near the aquarium and the popular Elli beach. All rooms have views of the sea or attractive 100 Palms Square. Restaurant and bar. Open March to December.

New Village Inn ✪ *Konstandopedos 110, 85100 Rhodes; Tel. (0241) 34937.* Excellent value, E-category pension situated in the heart of the New Town, just off Dragoumi and behind San Antonio Hotel. Quiet, clean, and secluded. Most rooms have ceiling fans.

Plaza Hotel ✪✪✪ *Ierou Lochou 7, 85199 Rhodes; Tel. (0241) 22501; Fax (0241) 22544.* B-category hotel in a central location, next to the Olympic Airways office. Four Seasons Restaurant, bar, coffee shop, pool, sauna.

Spartalis Hotel ✪✪ *N. Plastira 2, 85100 Rhodes; Tel. (0241) 24371; Fax (0241) 20406.* Simple, B-category hotel with bar, close to Mandráki Harbour.

Stella Guest House ✪ *Dilberaki 58, 85100 Rhodes; Tel. (0241) 24935; Fax (0241) 24935.* Friendly, comfortable, family-run guesthouse in a quiet street in the heart of the lively "cosmopolitan" district. All rooms have a balcony, and it's only a few minutes' walk to the beach. Some rooms with fridge and self-catering facilities. Air-conditioning on request.

Around the Island

Faliráki Beach Hotel ✪✪✪ *85100 Faliráki; Tel. (0241) 85301; Fax (0241) 85675.* High-standard, A-category hotel, with a good location on the beach. Offering 300 rooms, bars, restaurants, sea-water swimming pools, tennis facilities, and car hire. The popular Bistro serves snacks and meals all day.

Grecotel Rhodes Imperial ✪✪✪ *85101 Ixia; Tel. (0241) 75000; Fax (0241) 76691.* One of the newest hotels on the island, offering first-class accommodation and the range of amenities that go with it.

Líndos Bay Hotel ✪✪ *85000 Vliha Bay, Líndos; Tel. (0244) 31502; Fax (0244) 31500.* This superbly situated, A-category hotel is on quiet, sandy bay, 3 km (1½ miles) north of Líndos. Bars, restaurant, tennis facilities; hotel bus to Líndos.

Rodos Bay Hotel ✪✪✪ *85100 Ixia; Tel. (0241) 23662; Fax (0241) 21344.* The Rodos Bay has attained high standards for an A-category hotel, and offers 330 rooms, bars, restaurant, rooftop swimming pool, and convention facilities.

Rodos Palace Hotel ✪✪✪ *85100 Ixia; Tel. (0241) 25222; Fax (0241) 25350.* Luxury hotel with 610 rooms and bungalows. Private beach. Restaurants, bars, disco/nightclub, outdoor and indoor swimming pools, tennis, health centre. Everything from convention facilities to playland centre with extensive range of video computer games. Piano bar.

Symi

Aliki Hotel ✪✪✪ *85600 Symi; Tel. (0241) 71665; Fax (0241) 71655.* This tastefully restored waterside town house now offers charming accommodation, a pleasant restaurant, and a relaxed atmosphere.

Recommended Restaurants

Wherever you come from, you'll be amazed at the variety of restaurants in Rhodes Town, where you can sample cuisines from countries all over the world. Do not rely on the establishment's appearance as a gauge of quality, for you can eat extremely well in the most modest-looking taverna. On the whole, you're best to avoid those very smart restaurants sporting a tourist menu and dashing waiters to entice you inside with offers of free oúzo.

All establishments (with the exception of those in the luxury class) are price-controlled according to category. There is always a small cover charge and, although service charge is included in the bill, as a rule you're expected to leave a tip for the waiter. If a youngster brings iced water or cleans the table, it's customary to hand him a few drachmas as you leave. Despite these extras, prices are very reasonable—except for fish.

We appreciated the food and service in the restaurants listed below; if you find other places worth recommending we'd be pleased to hear from you.

To give you an idea of price (for a full meal with wine), we have used the following symbols:

✪	below 2,000 drs.
✪✪	2,000–3,000 drs.
✪✪✪	above 3,000 drs.

Rhodes, Old Town

Dodecanissos Taverna ✪✪✪✪ *Platía Evréon Martíron 45; Tel. (0241) 28412.* Best-value fish taverna in the Old Town and very popular among the locals. Fresh mussels, clams, and sea urchins daily. Grilled squid. Lunch and dinner.

Latino Ristorante ✪✪ *Ippodámou 11; Tel. (0241) 24876.* Excellent pizza and pasta, and a good selection of Italian wines. Open for dinner only.

Mike's Taverna ✪✪ *Menecléous 28; Tel (0241) 25359.* Greek food; music and dancing. Lunch and dinner.

Pithagóras Taverna ✪✪✪ *Pithagóras 22; Tel. (0241) 23711.* Seafood in a French atmosphere—strongly recommended for lobster.

Sotiris Taverna ✪ *Euripidou 4; Tel. (0241) 85148.* Through the archway on the right hand side of the supermarket in Platía Ippokrátous, where you'll find rickety tables and chairs in a little alleyway, and the creamiest *tsatsíki* in town. Open for lunch and dinner.

Tavérna Costas Hagicostas ✪✪ *Pithagóras 62; Tel. (0241) 26217.* Very good Greek food, particularly well known for fish dishes. Lunch and dinner.

Rhodes, New Town

Alatopipero ✪✪✪ *Mihaïl Petrídhi 76; Tel. (0241) 65494.* This *ouzerí* serves delicious meat and seafood specialities, plus more exotic dishes such as wild green crêpes and stuffed cyclamen leaves. Select wines from the region's micro-wineries are also on offer. Opens 6:30pm for dinner only; reservations recommended.

Aproupto Terverna ✪ *Kanada 95; Tel. (0241) 29096.* Specializing in *mezédes* (appetizers).

Christos Tavérna ✪ *Zephyros, Klaudiou Pepper Street; Tel. (0241) 31680.* Reliable taverna serving imaginatively created Greek dishes and good salads, such as beetroot with garlic, lettuce with spring onions. Tasty casseroles are always popular. Situated near Lomeniz Hotel. Lunch and dinner.

Rhodes

Kringlans Swedish Bakery ✪ *Amarandou 20; Tel. (0241) 20521.* The right place for a hearty, early breakfast—get there for opening time at 6am. Swedish filter coffee, fresh bread, croissants, honey-raisin buns, American cookies, and sandwiches with copious fillings.

Líndos Restaurant ✪ *Platía Vas. Pavlou; Tel. (0241) 24421.* Typical Greek taverna fare, served in very generous portions. Much used by locals. Open all day. Try the "Greek Plate" to get you started—it's the perfect introduction.

Palia Istoria ✪✪✪ *Mitropóleos 108; Tel. (0241) 32421.* One of the best tavernas in Rhodes; try the salmon with champagne sauce. Huge wine list. Dinner only; opens 7pm. Reservations essential.

Roumelli

Shere Khan ✪✪ *Orfanidou 52; no telephone.* The only Indian restaurant on the island. Creamy chicken *korma* and succulent *tandooris*, as well as the chef's speciality—*biriani*. Open for dinner only.

Around the Island

Anixis Taverna ✪ *Paradísi (opposite the airport); Tel. (0241) 91666.* Charming, family-run taverna in interesting old building with two trees growing through the roof. Delicious *stamnas* (veal and tomato stew), plus the purest spring water on the island.

Argo Taverna ✪✪✪ *Platía Ippokrátous 23-24; Tel. (0241) 34232.* Very popular, first-class seafood restaurant, overlooking the square. Be adventurous and try the squid stuffed with *féta* and herbs. The steaks are also good. A similar menu is offered by its sister taverna in Haraki (near Líndos). Open for lunch and dinner.

Baki Taverna ✪ *Émbonas Village Square; no telephone.* Simple, rustic taverna in Rhodes' wine capital. Excellent charcoal-grilled meats (choose your own cuts from the Baki Butchery), pan-fried liver in onions and wine, and the best salads on Rhodes. Characterful house wines, served in unlabelled bottles. Lunch and dinner.

Hermes Restaurant ✪✪-✪✪✪ *Líndos (near main square); no telephone.* Good all-round taverna, lunch or dinner. Classic Greek dishes, good wine list. Roof terrace.

Reni Fish Taverna ("O Afanis") ✪-✪✪✪ *Afántou Beach (southern end, near golf course); Tel. (0241) 51280.* Reputable for fresh fish. Delicious salads, mullet cooked on charcoal. Open all day.

La Rotisserie ✪✪✪ *Rodos Palace Hotel, Ixia; Tel. (0241) 25222.* French cuisine with regional specialities. Probably the best restaurant on the island.

Sandy Beach Taverna ✪ *Iályssos Bay; Tel. (0241) 94600.* Near the Sun Beach Hotel. Good choice of Greek salads, vegetables, and grilled meats. Delicious *keftédes* and *saganaki* (fried cheese). Waterside location. Open all day.

To Steki ✪ *Asgourou; Tel. (0241) 62182.* Classic *oúzeria* fare —choose a complete meal from an apparently limitless range of *mezédes* (appetizers). Evenings only. The retsina comes straight from the barrel.

Tzaki Taverna ✪ *Ixia; Tel. (0241) 26604.* On the main road, opposite the Roma Hotel. Wide range of Greek dishes, like *goúvetsi* and *kakavia* (fish soup). Barbecued lamb and charcoal-grilled steak and chops. Long-established and very popular with Greek families. Open all year round. Real log fire during winter. Live music, warm atmosphere.

ABOUT BERLITZ

In 1878 Professor Maximilian Berlitz had a revolutionary idea about making language learning accessible and enjoyable. One hundred and twenty years later these same principles are still successfully at work.

For language instruction, translation and inter-pretation services, cross-cultural training, study abroad programs, and an array of publishing products and additional services, visit any one of our more than 350 Berlitz Centers in over 40 countries.

Please consult your local telephone directory for the Berlitz Center nearest you or visit our web site at http://www.berlitz.com.

Helping the World Communicate